D1604555

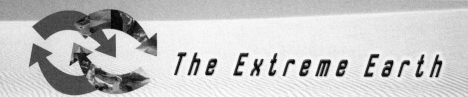
The Extreme Earth

Mountains

Peter Aleshire

Foreword by
Geoffrey H. Nash, Geologist

CHELSEA HOUSE
PUBLISHERS
An imprint of Infobase Publishing

To Ken Fink, who dreamed of being one of the geologists
who made the great discoveries recounted in this book
but who died in a helicopter crash chasing that dream

Chelsea House
An imprint of Infobase Publishing
132 West 31st Street
New York NY 10001

Library of Congress Cataloging-in-Publication Data
Aleshire, Peter.
  Mountains / Peter Aleshire ; foreword, Geoffrey H. Nash.
    p. cm. — (The extreme earth)
  Includes bibliographical references and index.
  ISBN-13: 978-0-8160-5918-8
  ISBN-10: 0-8160-5918-7
  1. Mountains—Juvenile literature. I. Title.
  GB512.A52 2008
  551.43'2—dc22
  2007020692

Chelsea House books are available at special discounts when purchased in bulk quantities for businesses, associations, institutions, or sales promotions. Please call our Special Sales Department in New York at (212) 967-8800 or (800) 322-8755.

You can find Chelsea House on the World Wide Web at http://www.chelseahouse.com

Text design by Erika K. Arroyo
Cover design by Dorothy M. Preston/Salvatore Luongo
Illustrations by Melissa Ericksen and Richard Garratt

Printed in the United States of America

VB FOF 10 9 8 7 6 5 4 3 2 1

This book is printed on acid-free paper and contains 30% post-consumer recycled content.

Contents

✧✧✧✧✧✧✧✧✧✧✧✦✧✧✧✧✧✧✧✧✧✧✧

Foreword	vii
Preface	ix
Acknowledgments	xi
Introduction	xiii

Origin of the Landform: Mountains — 1
The Formation of Mountains — 2
Ten Mountains — 2

1 ✧ Mount Everest, Asia — 4
A Mountain of Storms — 4
Mount Everest Facts — 5
More Deaths on the Mountain — 7
Measuring the Himalayas — 9
The Roots of the Mountain — 10
The Mallory Mystery — 12

2 ✧ Appalachians, North America — 14
A Mountain of Mystery — 15
The Sections of the Appalachians — 16
Agreeing on the Wrong Theory — 18
Rejected Theory Triumphs — 21
Origins of the Appalachians — 23
Geography Shapes History — 26
Mount Mitchell and Elisha — 28
The Appalachians's Mountain-building Periods — 28

3 ✧ The Alps, Europe — 31
Alps Reveal Deep Secrets — 32
Breaking Up Is Hard to Do — 35
Hypererosion Sets In — 37

Glaciers Apply Finishing Touch   38
Hannibal Succumbs to Geography   40

4 ✧ Mid-Atlantic Ridge, North Atlantic   42
Mid-Atlantic Ridge Validates Theory   42
World's Greatest Mountain Chain   47
Iceland Confirms Hot Spot Theory   50
The People of Mount Hekla   52
Volcano Threatens Town   53

5 ✧ The Sierra Nevada, California, the Western United States   55
A Series of Unfortunate Events   55
Mountains Reveal Continent's History   58
Yosemite: Wonderland of Granite   59
Glaciers Suppress Volcanoes   63
Ice Ages Sculpt Rocks   64
Heartbreaking Loss of the Second Yosemite   66
Lake Tahoe Warming Up   67

6 ✧ The Andes, South America   70
The Andes's Strangest Lake   70
Abrupt Rise Poses Mystery   71
Mystery Linked to the Mantle   73
The Inca Build a Complex Civilization   75
Worship   76
The Inca Create Mountaintop Civilization   76
Glaciers and Climate Change   77

7 ✧ Mauna Kea, Hawaii's High Point, Pacific Ocean   79
A Molten Mythology   80
The Best-studied Hot Spot   82
Yellowstone Hot Spot: A Titanic Explosion   83
A Volcanic Landscape   84
Mauna Kea: The Tallest Mountain   86
The First Hawaiians   87

8 ✧ Mount Saint Helens, Northwestern United States   89
Cascades: Edge of a Crustal Plate   89
Effects of Mount Saint Helens Eruption   92

A Violent History   94
An Explosive History of Mount Saint Helens   95
Cascades Support Plate Tectonics   96
Volcanic Mountains of the Cascades   97

9 ❖ Mount Kilimanjaro, Africa   100
The Shining Mountain   100
Glaciers in Full Retreat   104
Mountain Makes Its Own Weather   107
Kilimanjaro Life Zones   107
Great Rift Valley Shapes Continent   108
Age of Exploration   111
Mount Kenya   112

10 ❖ Humphreys Peak, Arizona, North America   114
Building a Mountain, One Eruption at a Time   115
Sunset Crater Phrase   117
The Unexpected Benefits of Disaster   121
Clues to a Vanished People   124

Glossary   127
Books   131
Web Sites   134
Index   137

Foreword

Mountains are a testament to the power of the opposing forces of nature—uplift and erosion. Many of the world's mountains exist as a result of the collisions between continental landmasses that have occurred over the 4.5 billion years since the Earth's formation. In fact, some mountains are still slowly rising and all mountains are gradually eroding. Careful scientific measurements document their rise but their erosion can be seen and understood with every grain of sand that washes down a ravine or every avalanche that roars down a mountain. Mountains have a special symbolism to many peoples and cultures. When asked why he wanted to climb Mount Everest, George Mallory, the early 20th-century mountain climber, is said to have famously replied, "Because it is there."

Mountains, one volume in the Extreme Earth set, introduces the reader to the geologic processes that have formed the mountain heights that have beguiled sightseers, climbers, and artists through our history. This book takes the reader to 10 of the most unusual mountains around the globe. These majestic landforms and the geologic processes that form them are introduced and many of their secrets are revealed. Some mountains are the result of continental uplift driven by plate tectonics and others are volcanic cones, built of lava rising from deep within the Earth. No matter their origin, they all stand out from their surroundings and demand attention.

Chapter 1 deals with Mount Everest in the Himalayas, the highest and most forbidding mountain in the world. Chapter 2 covers the Appalachian Mountains of the eastern United States, a much older, worn-down mountain range with an important part to play in the settlement of the continent by Europeans. These two mountain ranges, one relatively young and one older, provide the reader with a perspective on their geology and history. The Alps in Europe are discussed in chapter 3, in addition to the role they played in shaping the history of that continent when Carthaginian general Hannibal crossed them with his war elephants in 218 B.C.E., much to the surprise of Roman armies on the other side. Chapter 4 describes Iceland, which is a surface expression of the great chain of undersea mountains called the Mid-Atlantic Ridge. The discovery of this feature is one of the defining events in the theory of plate tectonics and Iceland sits astride this ever-turbulent rift in the Earth's crust.

Mountains discussed in later chapters include Mount Saint Helens in the Cascade Range of the northwestern United States, which provides a recent example of the power of volcanoes, and Mount Kilimanjaro in Africa, with its rapidly retreating glaciers due to global climate change.

Without the constant creation of new mountains through the process of plate tectonics, the forces of erosion would have long ago worn down the continents to sea level. Scientists only arrived at an explanation of mountain building about 50 years ago and there is still much for future scientists to learn. Author Peter Aleshire's book discusses the geology and history of mountains around the world and addresses issues ranging from the layers of ecosystems at various elevations to hazards posed by volcanic eruptions. With its useful glossary for those unfamiliar with some of the scientific terms, this book will be your reference to understanding the long, slow process that has brought about the mountain ranges we see today.

—Geoffrey H. Nash, geologist

Preface

From outer space, Earth resembles a fragile blue marble, as revealed in the famous photograph taken by the *Apollo 17* astronauts in December 1972. Eugene Cernan, Ronald Evans, and Jack Schmitt were some 28,000 miles (45,061 km) away when one of them snapped the famous picture that provided the first clear image of the planet from space.

Zoom in closer and the view is quite different. Far beneath the vast seas that give the blue marble its rich hue are soaring mountains and deep ridges. On land, more mountains and canyons come into view, rugged terrain initiated by movement beneath the Earth's crust and then sculpted by wind and water. Arid deserts and hollow caves are here too, existing in counterpoint to coursing rivers, sprawling lakes, and plummeting waterfalls.

The Extreme Earth is a set of eight books that presents the geology of these landforms, with clear explanations of their origins, histories, and structures. Similarities exist, of course, among the many mountains of the world, just as they exist among individual rivers, caves, deserts, canyons, waterfalls, lakes, ocean ridges, and trenches. Some qualify as the biggest, highest, deepest, longest, widest, oldest, or most unusual, and these are the examples singled out in this set. Each book introduces 10 superlative examples, one by one, of the individual landforms, and reveals why these landforms are never static, but always changing. Some of them are internationally known, located in populated areas. Others are in more remote locations and known primarily to people in the region. All of them are worthy of inclusion.

To some people, the ever-shifting contours of the Earth are just so much scenery. Others sit and ponder ocean ridges and undersea trenches, imagining mysteries that they can neither interact with nor examine in person. Some gaze at majestic canyons, rushing waterfalls, or placid lakes, appreciating the scenery from behind a railing, on a path, or aboard a boat. Still others climb mountains, float rivers, explore caves, and cross deserts, interacting directly with nature in a personal way.

Even people with a heightened interest in the scenic wonders of the world do not always understand the complexity of these landforms. The eight books in the Extreme Earth set provide basic information on how individual landforms came to exist and their place in the history of the planet. Here, too, is information on what makes each one unusual, what roles they play in the world today, and, in some cases, who discovered and named them. Each chapter in each volume also includes material on environmental challenges and reports on science in action, with details on field studies conducted at each site. All the books include photographs in color and black-and-white, line drawings, a glossary of scientific terms related to the text, and a listing of resources for more information.

When students who have read the eight books in the Extreme Earth set venture outdoors—whether close to home, on a family vacation, or to distant shores—they will know what they are looking at, how it got there, and what likely will happen next. They will know the stories of how lakes form, how wind and weather work together to etch mountain ranges, and how water carves canyons. These all are thrilling stories—stories that inhabitants of this planet have a responsibility to know.

The primary goal of the Extreme Earth set of books is to inform readers of all ages about the most interesting mountains, rivers, caves, deserts, canyons, waterfalls, lakes, ocean ridges, and trenches in the world. Even as these books serve to increase both understanding of the history of the planet and appreciation for all its landforms, ideally they also will encourage a sense of responsible stewardship for this magnificent blue marble.

Acknowledgments

Writers are like kids at concerts—they always have to sit on someone's shoulders to get a good view. This book would not have worked out but for the help of others, including geologist Geoff Nash, who did his best to protect me from foolish errors; executive editor Frank K. Darmstadt, who manages to coax a staggering number of books into existence; the editorial staff, including Melissa Cullen-DuPont and Alana Braithwaite; and Jeannie Hanson, who put the whole set together. I am also grateful to my wife for putting up with me and to my three sons for inspiring me to do better.

Introduction

A team of tourist-climbers obsessed with the need to stand on the world's highest place is instead scattered, battered, and finally frozen to death by a storm.

A general leading a great army of men and elephants stares towards the snow-clad peaks of the Alps, with the history of the Western world in the balance.

A geologist peers at smoldering Mount Saint Helens, eager to understand the deep forces of the Earth in the last moments of his life.

A party of immigrants takes the wrong path and so comes to a high ridge of the Sierra Nevada too late to force their path through its high passes. Trapped by the storm, the Donner Party struggles to survive—little knowing the horrors and descent into cannibalism that await.

A meteorologist, mocked by his colleagues for daring to suggest the solution to the most vexing geological mystery on the planet, freezes to death alone and defeated on the ice cap near the massive Mid-Atlantic Ridge; his theory will ultimately be confirmed and will revolutionize our understanding of the planet.

A geologist falsely mocked and rejected by his colleagues for his measurements of peaks in the Appalachians dies in a fall from the top of a waterfall that will bear his name, not knowing that modern techniques will validate him and restore his reputation.

An adventuresome geophysicist braves death repeatedly to finally lean over a volcanic vent high in the wilderness of the Andes to collect samples that will reveal deep secrets about the steepest, fastest-rising mountain chain on the planet.

A great magician bedecked in feathers and turquoise lays an offering of corn and prays in front of the advancing wall of molten rock that will first destroy everything he holds dear and then offer an ancient civilization an unexpected second chance.

A fervent missionary determined to save souls in the great unexplored expanse of Africa tops a ridge near the equator to see an astonishing sight—a gleaming, white-topped volcano that the native people

Morgan Harris, chairman of the Sierra Club Rock Climbing Committee, sits silhouetted atop the Diving Board in this 1937 photograph in Yosemite National Park. *(D. Brower, USGS)*

believe is inhabited by demons and a mysterious deadly force they refer to as "the cold." The snows of Kilimanjaro astonished the world when they were discovered and now have alarmed climate experts as they have disappeared.

Geologists in moon suits with special instruments flock to study the best-behaved volcanoes on the planet, which have built the world's tallest mountain in the form of the islands of Hawaii. They are drawn to this volcanic laboratory to understand the great, vital mystery of hot spots, which can persist for hundreds of millions of years and reveal the innermost workings of the Earth.

These are some of the stories offered in this book about 10 of the most unusual mountains on the planet. Of course, many other mountains and mountain ranges have equally fascinating human and geological histories, but these 10 peaks and mountain ranges have each shaped human and natural history, revealing the inner workings of the Earth. The brave, determined, reckless, foolish, triumphant, tragic stories of the people who have risked their lives to climb or study these remarkable mountains also reveal something of the intimate and vital connection between human beings and mountains. These great walls of rock and ice control patterns of settlement and trade, shape regional climate, and challenge human imagination. The generations-long effort by geologists to understand their origins and evolution has helped scientists understand the structure of the planet itself.

The following is a history of 10 captivating mountains and the strong, brilliant, sometimes doomed people who measured themselves against these peaks.

Origin of
the Landform

Mountains

The rise of mountains has long baffled geologists. What could account for these great upthrusts of rock rising miles from the average elevation of the surrounding land? What kept them tall and jagged, despite the steady erosion by wind and water?

Granted, even the tallest mountains on the planet seem puny when viewed from space. The greatest elevation change on the planet lies in the 100-mile (160-km) horizontal distance between the bottom of the Atacama Trench off the coast of Chile and the tips of the Andes Mountains that run along the coast—a 40,000-foot (12,200-m) change in elevation. That nearly nine-mile (14.5-km) change in such a short space seems impressive to us but is barely a bump on the surface of a planet with a 12,700-mile (20,440-km) diameter. In fact, if you shrank the Earth to the size of a billiard ball, the surface would feel just as glossy smooth—with a barely detectable nick here and there. Nonetheless, on a human scale, mountains demand an explanation.

Originally, geologists speculated that the cooling of a once-molten planet could account for both the great ocean basins and the tallest mountain ranges. For generations, geologists struggled to make this theory of mountain building work. They assumed that the rocks of the continents and the rocks of the ocean basins must differ in some way, and that they cooled at different rates. They speculated that as the crust cooled, it contracted—and the surface shriveled like the skin of a dried-out apple. Different rates of cooling based on the chemical compositions of the rock would cause ocean basins to contract more, while the rocks of the continents puckered up in the ridges of mountain ranges.

For many decades, most geologists would have agreed with this explanation for the rise of mountain ranges all over the planet. They published many complex, carefully constructed, laboriously measured theories and reconstructions to support this view of mountain building. However, the greatest strength in tackling a problem using the scientific method is that eventually the facts force the abandonment of incorrect theories. Those theories might result in great advances and shape decades of debate and investigation, but eventually the accumulation of better measurements and explanations will cause a shift in thinking. In this way, the great scientific theories focus, shape, and direct generations of those researchers striving to understand the universe.

THE FORMATION OF MOUNTAINS

In the case of the mystery of the formations of mountains, the theory of plate tectonics provided the vital framework to understand both the rise of mountains and the evolution of the surface of the planet. This once-radical and ridiculed theory suggests that the surface of the Earth is divided into great plates of thin, brittle crust. These light, hard surface rocks float on top of the very different, much deeper rocks of the Earth's *mantle*. Beneath the mantle lies the molten core of the planet. Geologists now believe that currents in the core are transmitted outwards into the much thicker mantle. That sets up currents in the mantle that reach up to the bottom of the thin crust of the surface. These currents have caused the crust to fracture into seven major crustal plates and many smaller, fragmented plates. These plates are created along *fissures* in the seafloor, where *magma* rises up to create great chains of undersea mountains like the Mid-Atlantic Ridge. This upwelling magma forces the plates on either side to move away from the ridge. Since the surface area of the Earth remains fixed, these moving crustal plates must go somewhere. So opposite every system of undersea ridges where new crust is manufactured lies a zone in which the same growing plate is destroyed. Such colliding plate edges either plunge down beneath the next plate in line or pile up in titanic head-on collisions with other plates.

TEN MOUNTAINS

These two alternatives account for most of the mountain ranges on the planet and for the division of this book. First, we will look at the mountain ranges caused by the head-on collision between two crustal plates. Such pile-ups of rock have raised the tallest and most massive mountain ranges on Earth. The latter part of this book examines volcanic mountains formed when volcanic hot spots cause an isolated mountain range in the middle of a crustal plate or when a buried crustal plate melts and fuels a volcanic chain of islands as the pressurized, melted magma escapes to the surface.

The surface of the Earth itself is essentially divided into two basic types of rock. First, most of the planet is covered by a dense, heavy layer of oceanic crust, mostly *basalt* and other volcanic rocks and magma. This dense igneous rock wells up along a great network of fissures running for thousands of miles, dividing the surface of the planet into seven major crustal plates. The upwelling of basalt that forms oceanic crust is driven by great convection currents at deeper levels. These great masses of heated, roiling, malleable rock form the bulk of the Earth's mass, kept hot and fluid by the decay of radioactive elements in the deeply buried rocks. The light, brittle crust of the Earth is a thin outer layer on this molten and semimolten mass of the hidden core and mantle layers, like the skin on a grape. Geologists believe this continual boiling in the Earth's core is transmitted outward through the rocks of the mantle and boil up against the underside of the crust.

Along the cracks in the crust that form the edges of the crustal plates, this molten rock pressing upward from below moves towards the surface, producing most of the planet's *volcano*es and earthquakes. As a result, new crust is continually created along these massive fissures in the seafloor, forcing aside the older rock. This creates a virtual geologic conveyor belt of rock as new magma forces apart plates along spreading centers. At the other end of the conveyor belt wait undersea trenches—the geological dark twins to the spreading centers of the undersea ridges. The trenches form where two oceanic plates press against one another and one gets forced down beneath the other. So the seafloor is mostly composed of this relatively young igneous rock, created at the spreading centers and driven back below the surface 50 million to 300 million years later deep beneath the trenches. So ocean crust is young, dense, volcanic rock.

The second type of rock at the surface of the Earth is geologically quite different and mostly forms the rock of the continents. Generally, the continental rocks are much lighter, varied, and older than the oceanic crust. In effect, the lighter rocks that comprise the continents are "floating" on top of the dense oceanic crust. Some portions of the continents are chunks of oceanic crust uplifted and stranded, but most of the continental rocks are lighter igneous and metamorphic rocks loaded with quartz and silica, or layered sedimentary rocks like sandstone, composed of layers deposited on shallow sea bottoms or valleys, then buried and fused. Once these rocks erupt onto the surface of the continents or get pasted onto the edge of an existing continent, they may remain at the surface for billions of years. That is why the oldest rocks on the seafloor are only a few hundred million years old, while the oldest continental rocks are nearly 2 billion years old.

The mountains of the Earth, therefore, are really the outward evidence of titanic forces. And that is why the study of these mountain chains has revealed deep truths about the evolution of the planet.

✧ **1** ✧✧✧✧✧✧✧✧✧✧✧✧✧✧✧✧✧✧✧✧✧✧✧✧✧✧

Mount Everest
Asia

Renowned mountain climbers Scott Fischer and Rob Hall planned their climbs to the top of the world's tallest mountain above sea level with exacting care. They had climbed so many of the world's most dangerous peaks, including Everest, that even relatively inexperienced climbers felt emboldened by having them along as guides to climb the 29,030-foot (8,850-m) mountain, a frozen jumble of rock forced five miles (8 km) upward by the devastating, slow-motion collision of continents. None of them knew that they stood on the brink of the most infamous tragedy in mountain climbing history, the perfect storm of miscalculation and bad luck, which horrified the world and underscored the strange and abiding human fascination with the struggle to reach the top of the mountain.

Few would have expected peerless climbers like Fischer and Hall to wind up at the epicenter of tragedy. Each led a separate expedition on that fatal day. An unprecedented eight climbers would die on the mountain that day. The disaster would achieve worldwide fame in part because writer Jon Krakauer happened to be in Hall's group and a film crew making an IMAX movie also got involved in the rescue. Krakauer's article for *Outside* magazine and his best-selling memoir *Into Thin Air* made the combination of bad luck and bad choices the subject of years of debate and controversy and opened a rare window into the drives, jealousies, and courage that drive men and women to climb the world's highest mountains.

A MOUNTAIN OF STORMS

Fischer and his guides Neal Beidleman and Anatoli Boukreev had considered every detail. They timed the push for the summit for the week of May 5–12, 1996, normally the best week to slip in between the howling storms of Everest and so reach the summit. Jutting into the planet-circling *jet stream* at an altitude that reduces the density of the

---

MOUNT EVEREST FACTS

The following is a list of interesting quick facts about the mountain:

- More than 2,238 people (as of the 2004 climbing season) have reached the top, half of them since 1998.
- Some 186 people have died trying to reach the top (as of 2004) and most of the corpses remain on the mountain because it is too dangerous to bring them down.
- The area above 26,000 feet (8,000 m) is considered the "death zone" where most climbers use supplemental oxygen.
- The revenue from the $25,000 permit to climb the mountain is a major source of income for Nepal.

---

air—and the oxygen—by a potentially lethal one-third, Everest draws to itself epic storms.

But on Thursday, May 9, the forecast for clear weather in the days ahead spurred the team to push for the summit from the holding pattern of the high, crowded base camp. Climbing through the calm, frigid night, the first team members reached the top on May 10 and gazed out across a staggering view. The climbers noted the gathering of clouds lower on the mountain, but Beidleman could not tell if they were the harbingers of a deadly storm. They resolved to hurry back to the base camp. On their way back down, the lead group passed the slower climbers guided by Fischer. (Fischer always remained with the slowest climbers to make sure they made it back down safely.) Delayed by a virtual traffic jam of other climbers ascending a difficult stretch with the help of permanently anchored ropes, Fischer's group knew they had to push hard to make the summit and get back down safely. Since each climber in his care had paid upwards of $65,000 for this once-in-a-lifetime chance to reach the peak, Fischer and Hall knew they had to deliver. The guides were paid $10,000 to $25,000 each, while the Sherpas who did much of the hardest work made about $2,000 each.

Beidleman later noted that Fischer seemed to be struggling against the climb and the altitude, but given Fischer's vast climbing experience Beidleman did not worry, considering how close to the peak they already were. But the winds rose to 75 miles (120 km) an hour by late afternoon, with snow flung sideways with such fury that the climbers could not see more than a few steps in front. Behind them in the storm, the climbers with Hall and Fischer were in an even more dangerous position.

Beidleman's team huddled together, sheltering one another from the killing wind and praying for the storm to pass, reluctant to take the risk of stepping off a cliff in the blinding white-out of the storm in the growing darkness. About midnight, the sky cleared enough for them to get their bearings from the appearance of the Big Dipper and the North Star. Shaking from the onset of *hypothermia*, Beidleman oriented himself with a glimpse of the peaks of Everest and Lhotse and with two of the stronger climbers made their way painfully back to base camp.

They found that Boukreev, Fischer's climbing partner, had also made it back to the base camp. Later, Boukreev would come in for fierce criticism when Krakauer suggested that he had endangered his clients by climbing without oxygen and pushing quickly back down from the summit. Boukreev later insisted that Fischer had approved his rapid descent, hoping he could come back with supplemental oxygen to help the last climbers down. For his part, Fischer stayed with the slowest climbers.

As soon as Beidleman arrived in camp, Boukreev set off back up the mountain to find the rest of Beidleman's party. They were stalled about 1,310 feet (400 m) from camp, slowly freezing to death near the infamous Kangshung face, a sheer 10,000-foot (3,050-m) drop on Everest's east side. Making numerous trips, Boukreev dragged or led team members back to camp. The whole team was back in camp by 4:30 A.M., with the exception of Fischer. The now nearly exhausted Boukreev made several attempts to climb back up to where Fischer had halted, connected by radio but immobilized by hypothermia and a lung disorder called pulmonary edema.

Climber Ed Viesturs told *Outside Online* that Boukreev made several attempts to climb after Fischer, but the weather was too severe and he had to turn back. Later, Krakauer would criticize Boukreev for not remaining with the inexperienced climbers on the summit with Fischer, suggesting he might have saved several of the eight climbers who died in various stages of the descent in the storm. Boukreev countered that he would have merely died along with Fischer, without being able to save several of the climbers.

Fischer had collapsed about an hour above camp. Sherpa Lopsang Jangbu was climbing with him and stayed with him, hoping he would recover enough to continue. Later, Lopsang would also contest Krakauer's account, which criticized him for climbing without oxygen and pushing on to the peak when the rest of the people in his struggling party turned back. Lopsang stayed with Fischer until the faltering expedition leader threatened to jump off a cliff if his companion did not continue without him. Lopsang reluctantly agreed, hoping he could reach camp and send back help. He left Fischer immobilized on a protected ledge and struggled painfully back to base camp. Clearly Fischer had been stricken by the effects of altitude sickness, which is responsible for most of the known deaths on Everest.

Hall's expedition had also stumbled onto disaster. In addition to guides Mike Groom and Andy Harris, Hall led an expedition of eight clients up the mountain. Slowed by the procession of 33 climbers attempting to reach the peak, they arrived at the top of the mountain an hour past the normal turnaround deadline. When one climber developed altitude sickness, Hall stayed behind to help him down. Trapped by the blizzard, Hall radioed for help. Harris headed back up with extra oxygen, only to vanish into the storm. Hall, Harris, and client Doug Hanson all froze to death in that terrible storm. Before he died, Hall talked to his pregnant wife by satellite phone, saying, "Sleep well my sweetheart. Please don't worry too much."

Meanwhile, an expedition made up of six members of the Indo-Tibetan Border Police was also trapped by the blizzard on the less-frequently climbed north face. Three climbers who earlier had turned back made it down, but the three who pushed on to the summit all died. Another controversial aspect of the tragedy was revealed the next day about a Japanese expedition that pushed on to the summit even after passing two nearly frozen members of the Indo-Tibetan Border Police expedition. The decision by the Japanese team not to attempt to rescue the doomed climbers was fiercely debated later.

Elsewhere on the mountain, rescuers set out to find Hall, Fischer, and the other missing climbers. Most of the rescuers were Sherpas, the native people of the high reaches of the Himalayas, essential to the current booming commercial exploitation of the mountain due to their superb physical conditioning and the enhanced oxygen-carrying capacity of their blood. When they finally reached Fischer, they were forced to make a cruel choice. They found Fischer in a coma, roped to Makalu Gao, a Sherpa left behind by the others when he fell ill from altitude sickness as well. Knowing they could only carry one climber down the treacherous slope, they took Gao because they were able to wake him from that slumber toward death. They bundled the unconscious Fischer warmly and left him with additional oxygen. By the time Boukreev reached Fischer later that day, the veteran guide had died. He was just one of eight climbers in three expeditions who died on the mountain during those two days. In fact, nearly one-third of the people who tackle Mount Everest die in the attempt, most often as a result of illness, exhaustion, or the cold on the way back down.

MORE DEATHS ON THE MOUNTAIN

Tragically, several years after surviving the mass deaths on Everest, Anatoli Boukreev died with one climbing companion in an *avalanche* on Christmas Day on Annapurna, another of the Himalayas' great peaks (26,700 feet [8,090 m]). A third man managed to ride the avalanche down the slope for some 800 feet (244 m), desperately swimming through the fluidlike, churning snow to the surface. Boukreev died still dogged by the controversy spurred by Scott Fischer's death, thanks to Krakauer's book, which suggested Boukreev first abandoned the clients struggling toward the summit then made heroic efforts to save them when it was too late. Boukreev had countered with his own account in his memoir *The Climb*. At the time of his death, Boukreev had already climbed seven of the 14 mountains on the planet higher than 26,250 feet (8,000 m) and was tackling Annapurna in the winter with light Alpine gear, a controversial trend in climbing that cuts against the traditional massive expeditions, laboriously staged ascents, and dependence on stashes of oxygen bottles in climbing the world's highest peaks. Lopsang, the Sherpa who tried so hard to save Fischer, also later died on the mountain. The 23-year-old Nepalese climber and two companions were swept away in an avalanche while working with an expedition from Japan. Lopsang, who climbed Everest four times without supplemental oxygen, died just months after Fischer.

Mount Everest has drawn such tragedy and controversy from the moment it was declared the world's highest mountain. Repeated efforts to reach the top in 1951 and 1952 turned back short of the summit. Edmund Hillary and Sherpa guide Tenzing Norgay were the first to climb it and survive. Hillary and Tenzing Norgay finally succeeded in May 1953, one of two teams in the same expedition that set out for the summit. News of the expedition flashed across the world, making Hillary an international celebrity.

Ironically, Hillary recently blasted the intense, competitive climbing culture for which he has become something of a patron saint. He expressed shock and dismay at reports that dozens of climbers, intent on making it to the summit, passed by British climber David Sharp, who lay slowly dying alongside the trail for lack of oxygen. Sharp, 34, ultimately died in his solo attempt to reach the summit. An estimated 40 climbers saw him alongside the now well-traveled route to the summit, without offering assistance. "Human life is far more important than just getting to the top of a mountain," Hillary told the New Zealand Press Association.

However, climbers on the mountain that day insisted Sharp was so close to death that no one could have saved him. In fact, bringing a helpless climber down from the summit would likely endanger the rescuers. That is why most of the people who have died on Everest remain frozen into the never-melting snow and ice, since the top of the mountain is too high for helicopters and a deadly hazard to anyone inside the thin air of the "kill zone." New Zealander Mark Inglis, the first double amputee to reach the mountain's summit on artificial legs, said a member of his party tried to give Sharp oxygen and sent out a distress call before heading on up to the summit. He insisted Sharp's condition, just 1,000 feet (300 m)

MEASURING THE HIMALAYAS

The slow-motion collision between two massive crustal plates that caused the towering uplift of the crumpled seafloor deposits that form the planet's highest mountains also can cause massive earthquakes. Now, geologists monitoring this ongoing, slow-motion geological train wreck are using it to understand fundamental forces in the Earth. Researchers have outfitted the Himalayas with a network of *Global Positioning System (GPS)* devices that measure position by triangulating satellite signals. The tiny changes in travel time between the measuring devices and the satellites overhead can be used to measure changes in position to a fraction of an inch. By anchoring the GPS measuring devices in the rocks atop the mountains, geologists can chart the ongoing movements of the crustal plates with unprecedented accuracy.

The measurements have helped geologists understand the detailed movements of the mountains. For instance, current measurements have revealed an ongoing warping of the mountain range, which may help explain the dynamics of major earthquakes in the region. In the past century, four major earthquakes have shaken the Himalayas, all exceeding 8 on the widely used Richter Scale—which makes them equivalent to the infamous 1906 San Francisco earthquake.

The network of brass or stainless steel pins is cemented into solid rock. Periodically, geologists remeasure the position of these pins, using satellite signals to set their position on the face of the Earth to within a tenth of an inch (2.5 cm). The change in the positions of these pins in relationship to one another gives scientists a measurement of how the mountain range is lifting, spreading, and warping.

The network has revealed that India continues to move northward at a rate of 0.7 inches (1.78 cm) each year, about one hundredth of the speed of the original collision between Asia and India that created the mountain range. The Himalayas, including Everest, continue to rise about 0.19 inches (.48 cm) per year. (See upper color insert on page C-1.)

Obtaining those measurements requires an exhausting scientific adventure, since geologists must climb to these high points each time they make fresh measurements. Periodically, the scientists hike with portable GPS receivers to each of the 26 survey points. The portable devices can pick up signals from eight different satellites orbiting the Earth at thousands of miles per hour at any one moment and calculate a precise location from the difference in travel time of the eight signals.

This satellite image from NASA shows the crumpling of the Himalayas, the opening rift of the Red Sea and much of western Asia, the world's largest continent comprising one-third of Earth's landmass. The raised mountain ranges are the result of a titanic collision between continents. *(USGS and NASA)* short of the summit, was hopeless. "I walked past David, but only because there were far more experienced and effective people than myself to help him," Inglis told the Associated Press. "It was a phenomenally extreme environment," with the temperature at the summit at 7:00 A.M. standing at -100°F (-73°C).

But Hillary bitterly criticized the new and harsher code of modern climbers, who on Everest in the few weeks of clear weather often line up for hours to climb past bottlenecks on the mountain. "There have been a number of occasions when people have been neglected and left to die and I do not regard this as a correct philosophy," Hillary told the *Otago Daily Times*. "I think the whole attitude toward climbing Mount Everest has become rather horrifying. The people just want to get to the top. It was wrong if there was a man suffering altitude problems and huddling under a rock, just to lift your hat, say 'good morning' and pass on by," he said. He said that his expedition "would never for a moment have left one of the members or a group of members just lie there and die while they plugged on towards the summit." More than 1,500 climbers have reached the summit of Mount Everest in the last 53 years and some 190 have died trying.

Perhaps it makes sense that the summit of Everest should inspire such blind, fatal, obsessive ambition, for it conceals beneath its glaciers, storms, and howling winds the astonishing, uplifted secrets to the evolution of the Earth. For Everest is the high point to one of the most violent, revealing, and remarkable landscapes on the planet. Consider just one mind-stunning fact about the highest place on Earth. Many of the rocks tilted toward heaven at the top of Everest are *limestone*, composed of the compressed skeletons of microscopic creatures that once lived in the bottom of a warm, shallow sea. Explaining this one remarkable observation requires a deep understanding of the violent and varied geological history of the world.

THE ROOTS OF THE MOUNTAIN

Some 250 million years ago, the surface of the planet was a very different place. Instead of seven continents scattered across the globe, the current-day landmasses of India, Africa, Australia, and South America were gathered together in a single equator-straddling supercontinent geologists have dubbed Pangaea. Pangaea existed for millions of years during the period when living species emerged from the nursery of the ocean and diversified into many forms on the land. But some 250 million years ago, just as the early dinosaurs were emerging for what would prove a 200-million-year run at dominating life on the land, forces deep inside the Earth began tearing Pangaea apart. *Rifts* developed in the middle of the massive continent, causing the landmasses that would eventually become most of the present-day continents to move apart. Pangaea essentially turned itself inside out, with the edges of the supercontinent becoming the collision zones of newly forming continents. Great masses of continental crust tore away from the parent continent as the rifts reached the surface and became spreading centers. That same process is taking place in the Red Sea today, opening up a rift between Africa and the Middle East that will one day probably gape open into a new ocean basin.

The dismemberment of Pangaea proceeded steadily. By about 60 million years ago, the chunk of crust that would eventually become India was an isolated island continent, much like modern-day Australia. For some reason connected to deep currents in the molten Earth, island India suddenly accelerated and shifted to the north. Geologists estimate India began moving at a geological breakneck speed of about six inches (15 cm) per year, according to a *Nova* television program written by Roger Bilham on the evolution of the Himalayas.

As India moved north on the crustal plate in which it was embedded, it overran the basin of the now extinct Tethys Ocean. This squeezed-out

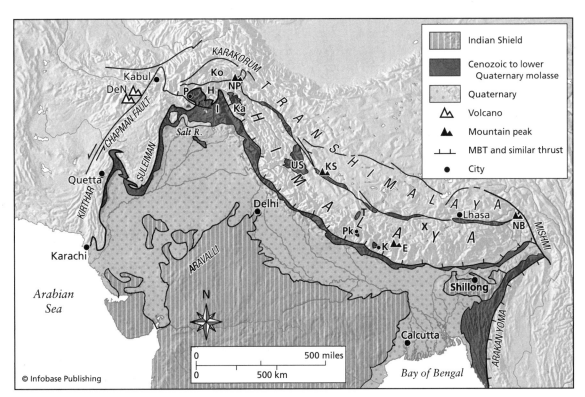

Simplified map of the Himalayas and surrounding regions. Abbreviations as follows: DeN: Dacht-e-Newar; E: Everest; H: Hazara; I: Islamabad; K: Kathmandu; Ka: Kashmir; Ko: Kohistan; KS: Kalais; NB: Namche Barwa; NP: Nanga Parbat; P: Peshawar; Pk: Pokhra; T: Thakkhola; US: Upper Sutlej; X: Xiagaze.

THE MALLORY MYSTERY

Sir Edmund Hillary won worldwide acclaim when he returned alive from the top of Everest, but he may not have been the first human being to reach it. The man many think reached the top first never got the credit, since he died on the mountain—the first of hundreds of people whose ambition to stand on the world's highest peak cost them their lives. Now, the fate of George Leigh Mallory is one of the mountain's most fascinating mysteries.

Mallory, 38, and Andrew "Sandy" Irvine, 22, set out to reach the summit in 1924, nearly 30 years before Hillary's successful attempt. Mallory had failed to reach the top in 1921 and 1922, which convinced him he had to bring bottles of oxygen—even though his tank and rig weighed a punishing 30 pounds (14 kg) and many of the bottles leaked. He enlisted the inexperienced Irvine to keep the then experimental oxygen bottles working and mounted yet another expedition. Mallory and Irvine set out from their high base camp at about 23,100 feet (7,040 m) on June 6, intending to spend three days getting to the top and back down. On the way up, they encountered another climber who loaned Mallory his camera, since the often-forgetful Mallory had left his at the base camp.

Geologist Noel Odell later caught a glimpse of two figures at a formation called the Second Step, near the base of the summit pyramid. This Second Step approach to the summit is considered difficult without anchored ropes, which Mallory lacked, but Mallory could climb on Irvine's shoulders to get past one otherwise impassable stretch. Odell noted they were lower than he would have expected after two days of climbing, but were moving steadily and seemed sure to reach the summit. Later in his life, Odell decided that perhaps the figures he had seen were only rock outcrops. That was the last time anyone saw Mallory or Irvine alive. Two days later, other members of the expedition hiked to Mallory's last high camp. They found hardware from the oxygen rig inside the tent, suggesting that Irvine had been tinkering with it. But the would-be rescuers could find no trace of the pair.

Ever since, climbers have sought clues that would reveal Mallory's fate. In 1933, climbers found an ice ax that might have been Irvine's on the route at 27,750 feet (8,460 m). Then, in 1975, a Chinese climber found the body of an Englishman some 750 feet (230 m) below the ice ax, with clothing so old it disintegrated at a touch. The Chinese climber, Wang Hongbao, died in a fall the day after he revealed his find to a friend and so never left precise information about the location of what could have been Irvine's body. Finally, in 1999, an expedition set out specifically to search for Mallory's body. First, they sought Irvine's body. They eventually did find the body and clear evidence of a fatal fall. But to their astonishment, the body proved to be Mallory's.

Not even the discovery of Mallory's body solved the central mystery: Did he make it to the top? Mallory's body was discovered well below the Second Step. One leading theory suggests that Mallory climbed on Irvine's shoulders at the Second Step and reached the summit, but had been so delayed by fiddling with the oxygen bottles early in the day that he had to come down in the darkness. That prompted him to avoid the Second Step and detour to the route where he finally fell and died. Irvine likely waited for him in vain at the bottom of the Second Step then died of exposure trying to get back down on his own. A climber found a body likely to be Irvine's in 1960, but subsequent expeditions have been unable to locate the body again. However, many other climbers believe that the sighting of Mallory above the Second Step was actually at the much lower First Step and that Mallory never reached the summit. Only one piece of evidence will likely settle the question—Mallory's borrowed camera, still buried in the snow. Perhaps it holds an image from the top of Everest that will prove Mallory was the first person to stand atop the world's highest place. In the meantime, he will be remembered for being the first to utter the quintessential explanation for why climbers risk their lives to reach the peak: "Because it's there."

ocean basin is the source for the layered sedimentary rock found now on top of Everest and the other great peaks of the Himalayas. Eventually, the movement of the Indian plate entirely consumed the ocean basin. Then, the continental rocks slammed directly into Asia. India pressed north, its movement slowed by a deep connection to a chunk of buried ocean floor, which acted like a great anchor. Some 25 million years ago, the collision began to crumple and fold the rocks, like cars in a head-on collision. Instead of letting the leading edge of the Indian plate slide down under the Asian plate, the collision began to create the planet's highest mountain range.

Some 10 million years ago, the mountain-building collision was in full force, generating such powerful resistance that it ruptured the connection between the light continental crust of India and the heavy anchor of the attached *oceanic crust* still descending beneath Asia. The remains of the Indian plate vanished deep beneath Asia, leaving the scrapings of the one time island continent pasted to the edge of the Asian plate in the form of the Himalayas.

Geologists do not fully understand exactly what happened next. Somehow, the deep forces working on the crustal plates shifted. The Indian continent was driven beneath Tibet like a giant wedge, which forced Tibet sharply upward, making the Tibetan Plateau and the Himalayas the most dramatically uplifted area on the planet. This process should continue for the next 5 to 10 million years, as India plows another 112 miles (180 km) into Tibet.

Appalachians

North America

One could easily overlook the Appalachian Mountains and dismiss them as mere hills, the worn, rolling nubs of mountains. This rambling 100 to 300 mile (160–480 km) wide, 1,500 mile (2,410 km) long chain of overlapping mountain ranges reaches its high point at the 6,680 foot (2,040 m) summit of Mount Mitchell in North Carolina—half the height of even average peaks in the Rocky Mountains and only a quarter the height of Mount Everest. Although Mount Mitchell ranks as the highest point in the eastern United States, most of the mountain chains that together form the Appalachians reach to barely 3,000 feet (910 m) in height.

Although the streams and rivers of the Appalachians seem modest now, they have worn down a mountain range that was once probably a match for the Himalayas. *(USGS)*

And yet, the study of the Appalachians can yield clues to the long history of the planet, for the worn and eroded of peaks of this long mountain range once rivaled the Himalayas and in their folded and tormented layers reveal the long history of the planet. Solving the mystery of their formation and the seemingly inexplicable connection to a mountain range in Africa provided a key element in the development of the theory of plate tectonics that revolutionized the understanding of geology.

Moreover, the geographic barrier of the Appalachians shaped the history of the United States more than perhaps any other single landform. This layered chain of mountains with only scattered passes confined initial settlement of the United States to the broad coastal plain between the foothills of the Appalachians and the Atlantic Ocean. Most of the original thirteen colonies developed in that broad area, ensuring enough continuity, density of population, and stability to foster the development of the United States of America, in contrast to the dispersed settlement patterns beyond those mountains where French explorers and settlers never built a colony to rival the areas to the east of the Appalachians.

A MOUNTAIN OF MYSTERY

Early geologists trying to account for the evolution of the Appalachian Mountains in the 1800s and early 1900s had a mystery to tackle. (See lower color insert on page C-1.) Clearly, the Appalachians were the remains of an ancient mountain system—contorted, folded, and worn. The scientists had mapped all of the warped and folded layers, ancient sea bottom *sediments* that had been buried, fused, and metamorphosed into new rocks. Then those rocks had been uplifted great distances and intermingled with the outpours of many *volcano*es. Finally, the uplifted mountains had been worn down again, leveled by the relentless erosion of water, ice, and wind. All that seemed apparent from the sequence of rock layers. Geologists could even account for the great mass of rock that had been eroded off those once great peaks. These loose, eroded sediments were piled miles deep onto the coastal plain of the United States, a broad, low-lying region several hundred miles wide running down the whole eastern edge of North America.

Now here is the mystery. The sediments of the coastal plain and the underwater continental shelf were piled so deep that they had to have accumulated in a broad, low-lying region between two mountain ranges. If they were not trapped in a gigantic basin, they would have simply washed out to sea. So what happened to the other half of the basin? What happened to the parallel chain of great mountains necessary to trap the miles of sediment eroded off the crest of the Appalachians? For many decades in the early 20th century, geologists could only shrug and continue chipping away at a host of mysteries shrouding the evolution of mountains. In

---

THE SECTIONS OF THE APPALACHIANS

Today, the Appalachians are generally divided into the following four sections:

+ The Piedmont, a plateau, 450–900 feet (140–270 m) above sea level, extending from Alabama to New York consisting of crystalline metamorphic and igneous rocks first formed in the *Paleozoic* between 540 million and 250 million years ago. The originally seafloor sedimentary layers and volcanic ocean crust were buried, heated, and reformed into a variety of metamorphic *schists* and slates, with granite intrusions and belts of serpentine.

+ The Blue Ridge forms a narrow, mountainous zone of hard Proterozoic (500 million to 1 billion years old) rocks that divides the Piedmont from the inland Valley and Ridge Province. Created by a fault zone that transported rocks and layers from great distances, this boundary zone made mostly of sedimentary rocks created both beautiful mountains and a barrier for travel between the coast and the interior of the continent.

+ The Valley and Ridge Province is comprised of heavily folded and deformed Paleozoic sedimentary rocks that have formed great anticlines, in which layers bow upward, and synclines, in which layers bow downward. The complex, upended, and folded layers of sedimentary rock created the distinctive valley-ridge landscape that defines the Appalachians and that made them a major barrier despite their modest height.

+ The Appalachian Plateau sits on top of gently folded and largely undeformed Paleozoic sedimentary rock layers. Streams have cut deeply into the relatively soft layers, creating a rugged terrain that made travel from the east to the west very difficult. Most of the mountains in this zone are comprised of metamorphic rocks, with frequent intrusions of volcanic deposits.

---

fact, they did not have any strong theories on how mountains developed. What caused one chunk of the Earth to rise to 28,000 feet (8,530 m)? No one knew for sure.

Early philosophers argued that the mountains, valleys, and other remarkable features of the Earth were signs of the great flood of the Bible. They argued that God would have created the Earth as a perfect sphere, but that the tremendous flood with which the Creator scourged the Earth in anger at human behavior gouged out great valleys and canyons and piled up high mountains. Philosophers continued to advance and research such ideas into the 1800s.

But others sought explanations for the rise of mountains that did not rely on divine intervention. Jean-Baptiste Élie de Beaumont, a French geologist, in 1852 suggested that mountains were forced upward when rocks were squeezed as in the "jaws of a vise," although he offered no clear explanation for what might be causing the squeeze. At that time, many geologists argued that the Earth was gradually cooling, causing it to contract as it cooled. This contraction was thought to have caused the surface of the Earth to crack and wrinkle. The cracks became valleys and low-lying regions and the wrinkles became mountain ranges.

The first well-developed form of this theory stemmed from the work of American scientists attempting to explain the rise of the Appalachians. James Hall and James Dwight Dana working with the rocks of this crucial mountain range in the mid-1800s were the first to use the term *geosynclinal* in discussing the gradually deepening and filling basin alongside the Appalachians. These pioneering geologists eventually concluded that the existence of the deep basin filled with sediment alongside the mountain chain was evidence of the gradual cooling and contracting of the Earth.

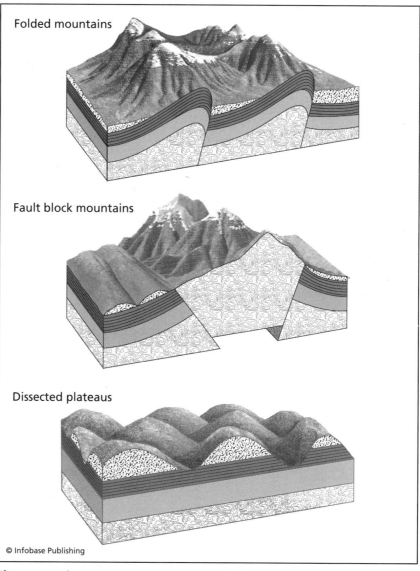

Folded mountains

Fault block mountains

Dissected plateaus

© Infobase Publishing

Three mountain types

Seeking to explain the great difference between the low-lying ocean basins and the uplifted continents with their great mountain chains, Dana argued that as the Earth cooled the continents formed first, since they were made of quick-cooling rocks like quartz and feldspar. The ocean basins developed more gradually, since they were made of slower cooling olivine and pyroxene. The different cooling rates caused different rates of contraction, accounting for the deep ocean basins and the high-riding continents. The theory could even explain the giant mountain ranges that run along the edge of many continents, like the Andes and the Himalayas. Surely, those mountain ranges had puckered up along the margins between the quick-cooling continents and the slow-cooling ocean basins, like the seams on a dress.

AGREEING ON THE WRONG THEORY

Other geologists argued that the ocean basins were left over from a catastrophic event that took place as the molten Earth cooled. The spin of the Earth had perhaps set up waves in the still-molten rock. The waves circled the globe, building up on top of each other. At some point, just as the Earth's surface solidified, this rotation-driven wave of semimolten rock ripped loose a great chunk of the Earth, which spun off into space. That created the Moon and left behind a great hole, which became the first ocean basin.

Despite the continued problems with these explanations, most geologists explained mountain building through some version of Dana's concept of a geosyncline, a trough gradually filled with eroded sedimentary rock that was compressed, deformed, and then built up into a mountain range, largely through the activities of volcanoes which caused the crust to expand and laid down new layers of rock. This was the beginning of a complicated theory intended to explain the buildup of mountains and the frequent discovery of rocks at lofty heights that had been created on ocean bottoms. Other geologists added details to the theory of geosynclines, providing masses of detailed measurements and observations of the strange jumble of rocks of different types brought together in a single mountain range.

Eduard Suess (1831–1914), an expert on the Alps in Europe, was a brilliant young scientist who first published important papers and speculations when he was just 19 and went on to strongly influence the development of geology while a professor at the University of Vienna. He began gathering the first baffling clues to the unexpected connections between distant mountains and the existence of vanished seas and oceans, left behind in the form of layers of ocean-bottom mud fused into rock and mysteriously moved miles from any likely locations of a seafloor.

In the mid-1800s, he presented intriguing evidence that the mountains of Africa and Europe were once connected, based on the continuation of certain distinctive rock layers from one mountain range to the next, despite the presence of the Mediterranean Sea in between. Moreover, he argued that rocks now on top of the Alps had been laid down originally on the bottom of the Mediterranean. He supported the earlier geosyncline theory, but his evidence showing baffling connections between distant mountain ranges had important consequences for the ensuing history of geology. For instance, he discovered the fossil remains of the *glossopteris* fern in rocks of South America, Africa, and India. This prompted him to propose that the three distant land masses were once connected in a supercontinent he dubbed *Gondwana (Gondwanaland)*. He argued that continuous mountains once connected three of the existing continents, but that oceans had flooded into the intervening space. However, picturing such a mountain zone and the resulting intrusion of an ocean offered almost as many problems as it solved, although Seuss was right to focus on the match-up of layers and fossils in widely separated mountain ranges.

Eventually, the fossils and rock layers would include intriguing evidence of a precise match between the Appalachians and the Atlas Mountains of Africa. The Atlas Mountains extend through Morocco, Algeria, and Tunisia and include the Rock of Gibraltar. Strangely enough, the sequence of layers and the fossils found in the rocks of the Atlas Mountains bear an uncanny resemblance to the same sequences and fossils in the Appalachians, although the highest peaks of the Atlas Mountains still reach a height of 13,670 feet (4,170 m). Moreover, geologists have also established a match between the Appalachians and the Sierra Nevada in Spain.

As field research demonstrated many such puzzling connections between the rocks of mountain ranges on different continents, geologists struggled for an explanation. The Atlas Mountains seemed to provide the other wall of that flat Atlantic Plain, piled miles deep with sediments eroded off the surrounding mountains. But how could geologists account for the intervening Atlantic Ocean, with uncharted depths reaching downward into the darkness for miles? How could the shrinking and cooling of the Earth have swallowed up thousand of miles of vanished mountains that might have once connected the Appalachians and the Atlas Mountains?

The revolutionary answer to that question would eventually emerge from the work of German meteorologist Alfred Lothar Wegener (1880–1930), who struggled to devise a comprehensive theory to explain the confusing field observations of generations of geologists. An adventurer and a scientific dabbler, Wegener's original scientific training was in astronomy, which led him to research on climate. He used hot air balloons in an innovative experiment to trace wind currents in the upper *atmosphere* and trudged across the vast expanse of ice in Greenland as he developed a theory on how climatic changes at the top of the world generated weather all over the planet. His restless and unconventional intellect soon led him to focus on the growing mass of research on the strange match between rock layers and fossils in mountain ranges on widely separated continents, including the strong evidence connecting 300-million-year-old rock layers on both sides of the Atlantic and the discovery of the fossils of tropical plants on the Arctic island of Spitsbergen.

Wegener came up with a bold idea. Suppose the continents used to all huddle together in some kind of great, squashed-together supercontinent? Eduard Suess had proposed the existence of such a continent much earlier, but he had theorized that somehow all the intervening mountain ranges had dropped into the basin that became the Atlantic Ocean, perhaps as a result of the cooling of the Earth. Wegener could not reconcile such a great change in the surface of the Earth with any measured cooling effect. So he suggested that somehow this supercontinent had split up and North America had moved to the east while Africa and Europe moved west, drifting to their present locations. The rocks matched because they were made at the same time in the same place before splitting up. The fossils matched because 300 million years ago Europe, North America, South America, Africa, Australia, Asia, and even Arctic islands were all part of a single, giant continent on which the dinosaurs first arose somewhere near the equator.

The experts generally dismissed Wegener's theory. Other people had noticed the strange match of fossils of a certain age all over the world, but they figured that land bridges once connected the continents, stretching across the oceans, just like the Bering Strait up by Alaska. Maybe those hidden land bridges rose to become dry land during ice ages, when sea levels dropped hundreds of feet all over the world because so much water froze into ice at the poles. This would allow animals to move from continent to continent along land bridges that subsequently sank beneath the ocean, argued the fossil experts. After all, you could hide almost anything in the ocean, which covered three-quarters of the Earth's surface.

Drafted into the German army when Word War I broke out, Wegener was badly wounded during one of the bloody battles on the western front. During his long months of recovery in the hospital, he thought ceaselessly about his theory. When he recovered, he became an army weatherman. After the war, Wegener returned to the University of Berlin to finish work on his theory of "continental drift," which he first published in 1915 and expanded on in 1920, 1922, and 1929. He called the great, vanished continent Pangaea, which in Greek means "all the Earth." According to Wegener, Pangaea broke up some 300 million years ago, and the pieces moved away from each other at a speed of about 10 inches (25 cm) per year, like icebreakers plowing through the ice.

Most experts initially dismissed his theory, since he could offer no physical explanation as to how the rocks of the continents could somehow move across the rocks of the seafloor like drifting icebergs. He suggested the spin of the Earth or the gravitational pull of the Moon might provide the energy, but his critics rightly pointed out that if those forces had the power to make continents drift they would also have torn the Earth apart—or at least jumbled the layered geological connections between continents on which his theory depended.

Granted, some geologists cautiously suggested that bumper-car continents might explain the remarkable crunched-up rock layers of the Alps and the jigsaw puzzle pattern of the fossils, but most scientists dismissed the theory as physically impossible. Geologists, especially American geologists, agreed that a good theory should emerge from a mass of observations, rather than spring out of the head of a weatherman. Spurned by his colleges, Wegener returned to his first obsession, understanding polar weather patterns. He returned to Greenland in 1930 to study the weather there. When another group of scientists got stranded on the ice, Wegener led an expedition to bring them food. Tragically, he died on the return trip, a creative scientist rejected by the experts.

REJECTED THEORY TRIUMPHS

However, in the ensuing decades, additional evidence gathered from the seafloor would prove Wegener correct and revolutionize geology by demonstrating that the Appalachians and the Atlas Mountains once formed a single mountain range in the midst of Wegener's proposed supercontinent. Wegener's vindication had to wait on further discoveries that could explain how these great masses of rock could apparently break up and move apart to end up separated by thousands of miles and a deep, wide ocean.

Several widely divergent lines of evidence would eventually converge to explain this mystery, which proved central to the whole evolution of the surface of the Earth. One key development was the ability to map the topography of the seafloor, which was spurred by World War II and the development of sonar to locate and destroy the submarines that were attacking convoys in the Atlantic Ocean. Scientists learned to bounce sound waves off the seafloor and create images of the terrain far beneath the surface. These sonar images, combined with soundings of the seafloor, revealed a great chain of mountains running up the middle of the Atlantic Ocean, later termed the Mid-Atlantic Ridge. The greatest mountain range in the world, the 12,000-mile (19,300-km)-long chain of undersea mountains connects to a ridge system that covers a quarter of the Earth's surface and continues for some 42,000 miles (67,600 km), with a width of 600 to 2,500 miles (970 to 4,000 km). Along most of its length, a mile-deep (1.6 km) rift runs along the crest of the ridge. Decades of measurement eventually demonstrated that the Mid-Atlantic Ridge is a giant fissure in the Earth, into which *basalt* constantly wells—causing the development of earthquakes and undersea volcanoes and forcing apart the young, heavy oceanic crust on each side of the rift.

The key to this insight was the discovery that magnetic elements in molten rock align themselves with the Earth's magnetic poles as the molten rock cools. Moreover, geologists also discovered that the Earth's magnetic poles periodically flip, changing their alignment so that a compass that once pointed north would point south. Therefore, the magnetic elements that froze into place in fresh lava would point in the direction of the magnetic poles at that moment—sometimes north, sometimes south. Once geologists precisely measured the times in the past when the Earth's magnetic field had reversed itself, they had a way of calculating the age and position of once-molten rock. This discovery provided the clue to another riddle, perplexing magnetic stripes on each side of the Mid-Atlantic Ridge. These broad stripes ran for great distances, with a mirror-image pattern on each side of the ridge. These stripes were created by the cooling of a long swath of molten rock at the center of the ridge, which had then been split in two and moved away from the ridge.

This insight provided the crucial measurement needed to vindicate Wegener, confirm the theory that the surface of the Earth is divided into gigantic crustal plates, and incidentally make it possible to reconstruct the history of the Appalachian Mountains. This theory of plate tectonics demonstrates that the surface of the Earth is divided into at least seven major plates of light crustal rock and many smaller ones. Most of the plates are composed of dense, basaltic oceanic crust, floating on top of the semimolten rock of the Earth's *mantle*. The mantle, in turn, surrounds the much smaller molten core. Heated by the natural *radioactivity* of rocks, vast *convection* currents in the molten core and semimolten mantle constantly press up against the cool, hard rock of the Earth's thin crust. These currents crack and shift those crustal plates. The Mid-Atlantic Ridge forms the most prominent crustal plate edge on the planet. The rifting of the Earth more than 200 million years ago that created the Mid-Atlantic Ridge also split apart Pangaea and began the long separation of the Appalachian and Atlas Mountains. The theory of plate tectonics made sense of a host of deep mysteries and enabled geologists to piece together the complex history of the Appalachian Mountains, from their folded, seafloor rocks to the deposition of the coastal plain.

ORIGINS OF THE APPALACHIANS

The story of the Appalachians started some 480 million years ago in shallow seas on the edge of a quiet continent. At that time, very few creatures of any sort lived on the land. Nearly all life was concentrated in the oceans, mostly simple organisms. The skeletons of microscopic creatures that died and settled into the mud eventually created great layers of limestone. But violent times lay ahead for those quiet layers of buried sediment. The deep current driving the movement of the crustal plates and their embedded continents now began to assemble most of the scattered island continents into a single great mass—Pangaea.

Between 440 and 480 million years ago the mass of rock that would eventually become North America drifted into collision with the edge of another crustal plate. One of two things happens when two crustal plates collide, smashed against one another by the rise of *magma* along a spreading center like the Mid-Atlantic Ridge. Either they crumple and shove against one another, which raises a massive mountain range like the Himalayas, or one plate is forced down under the other. When the latter happens, the front edge of the plate on the bottom slides down underneath the uppermost plate. As the rocks of the descending plate get deeper, they heat up and eventually melt. This creates a zone of pressurized, molten rock relatively near the surface. This molten rock finds its way to the surface along cracks and *fissures* in the stressed, overlying crustal plate. This in turn, generally spurs an era of violent and prolonged volcanic activity along the edge of the overlying plate.

That is exactly what happened when the smaller plate was forced down beneath the North American plate. The Appalachians were born in this creation of a subduction zone. Not only did the volcanoes caused by the descending plate spew new layers of rock onto the surface, but the jostling of the massive crustal plates caused extensive faulting and uplift of both the layers of limestone and the new layers of volcanic ash and lava. Immediately, erosion set in—tearing down the rising mountain range as it was built.

This was just the first in a complicated series of eruptions and mountain building episodes that persisted for the next 250 million years as the shifting of crustal plates assembled Pangaea from many scattered parts. This process of assembly and destruction happens constantly on the surface of the Earth as fresh crust is created at a spreading center, moves outward on the conveyor belt of the crust and is eventually consumed in a subduction zone. The continents are mostly bystanders and witnesses to this process, since the light rock of the continents effectively "floats" atop the dense rock of the oceanic crust. Often when crustal plates clash, the light continents are left behind—effectively scraped off the top of a descending crustal plate.

This ceaseless plate movement, with its spectacular creation and destruction of the crust, seems to randomly gather together the continents every 400 to 500 million years. Some 250 million years ago, it resulted in the assembly of Pangaea. The final stage in the assembly of the supercontinent was the collision with ancestral Africa or Gondwana. Now close to the equator, Pangaea had gathered up nearly all the continental crust on the planet with the ancestral Appalachians pushed up to imposing heights in the very center. At this point, the great peaks of Appalachians, Atlas and other now scattered mountain ranges were gathered into a single great wall of upthrust rock, much like the Himalayas of today.

By now, life had spread across the surface of the Earth, as evidenced by the fossil traces found in the rocks of the Appalachians. Some 200 million years ago, the first dinosaurs were emerging for their 150-million-year long dominance of life on the continents. The fossils from that period demonstrate that the dinosaurs wandered across a vast, assembled landmass lying astride the equator. This great continent fostered the spread and evolution of the dinosaurs and helps account for the close match now in the fossil finds on scattered continents, including North America and Africa. The great saurians did not have to wander through polar regions and cross fickle land bridges; they wandered a great continent with no winters save on the very tops of the massive mountains ranges, like the ancestral Appalachians.

But change remains the one constant on the restless Earth. Soon, the same forces that had assembled Pangaea began to rip it apart. Driven by those same deep currents in the mantle, a new rift system that would one day spawn the Mid-Atlantic Ridge opened up about 220 million years ago in the middle of Pangaea, dividing the ancestral Appalachians and beginning the long scattering of its once connected layers of rock. Moreover, the violent shifting in the plate margins cut the mighty Appalachians off from the upwelling volcanoes of the plate margin that had created them. Moving away from the uplift and violence of the plate margin as it drifted off to the west, the Appalachians no longer had the volcanic activity and uplift that had built them to such great heights. Now, only relentless erosion shaped the range. As the shift of the continents separated the Appalachians from the retreating Atlas Mountains, the vast quantity of sediment eroded from the summits of the mountains built up in the rift between them, laying the foundations of what would become the North American coastal plain.

By the end of the Mesozoic era some 65 million years ago, the once lofty mountain chain had been worn down to a nearly flat plain. By then, the continents had separated into a recognizable version of their current forms. The dinosaurs were nearly all extinct. However, the Appalachians were not quite done, despite the violence of their birth and the long wearing of their dismantlement. In the past 65 millions years, as North America drifted further into its present location, the currents deep beneath the surface yielded another period of uplift for the deformed, re-heated, buried, and re-risen rocks of the Appalachians. A fresh era of uplift brought those old, basement layers of recrystalized limestone back to the surface. The massively folded sedimentary layers were upended in strange configurations, like a throw rug that has been bunched up until the folds fall on top of one another. These upended layers, when subjected to renewed erosion, have given the Appalachians their current striking topography.

As magma was forced up along the great rift of the Mid-Atlantic Ridge, the Atlantic Ocean steadily widened and the Appalachians moved farther away from their sundered half left behind in northern Africa and southern Europe. Layers of marine sediments that had once been buried, dramatically folded and uplifted were mingled with layers of lava and slivers of ocean crust as the geologically violent events unfolded. Some of those folded layers of former marine sediment included millions of years of accumulated organic sediment from the bottoms of swamps and inland seas. Buried and subjected to intense heat and pressure, these layers of organic debris were eventually fused and heated and re-cooled into great layers of coal.

As North America drifted to its current position, the modern form of the Appalachians began to take shape. The extensively folded layers of metamorphosed marine sedimentary layers formed a variable, 1,500-mile (2,410-km)-long barrier along the edge of the continent. To the west, the miles-deep deposits of debris washed off the once lofty peaks of that mountain range and formed the Atlantic Plain, stretching from Cape Cod some 2,200 miles (3,540 km) through the southeast United States and down to the Yucatan Peninsula in Mexico. Along with much of Florida, this flat area filled with sediments eroded off the once-mighty Appalachians is referred to as the Gulf Coastal Plain. A portion of this broad, relatively flat plain is underwater and constitutes the continental shelf offshore of the coast.

Renewed uplift of the Appalachians in the past 65 million years created the current landscape. As the mountains shifted upward, streams regained their erosive energy. These streams cut through the limestone and *shale* layers down toward the ancient bedrock. All told, some 30,000 feet (9,000 m) of heavily folded Paleozoic sedimentary layers ended up piled on top of the Appalachians, only to be nearly entirely removed by erosion.

Many of those streams cut through the softer marine layers, especially when those layers had been tilted upwards like a deck of playing cards stood on its side. These layers turned edgewise proved especially yielding to erosion. However, peculiarities of layering and topography sometimes generated streams powerful enough to cut through even the bedrock layers. This final phase of uplift and erosion cut gaps through the great folded layers of the mountain that separated the coastal plain from the interior for a stretch of nearly 2,000 miles (3,200 km).

GEOGRAPHY SHAPES HISTORY

The steep, parallel ridges of the Appalachians formed by the tilted layers of rocks that once lay on seafloors half a world away had a fundamental impact on the course of the history of the United States. For a century, the north-south trending wall of mountain ridges confined the British effort to colonize the New World to the Atlantic Coastal Plain. The multiple ridges and valleys that extend north to south, as well as the heavy forest and dense undergrowth, all held settlers to an area between the coast and the foothills of the mountains. The only good path through the mountains lay through the Hudson and Mohawk Valleys or by going around the southern end of the range through present-day Alabama. Powerful confederations of Indian tribes for a long time laid secure claim to those few east-west running valleys, and Spanish settlements to the south also limited the migration of British colonists.

But what seemed a disadvantage actually proved vital in determining the future of the continent. The French, who claimed most of the interior west of the Appalachians, established a network based on trading and fur trapping rather than settlement, partly because of the difficulty of supplying colonists in that great wilderness. The British settlements along the coast, by contrast, became dense, developed, and prosperous. In some areas, accidents of geography based on the tilting and erosion of those ancient layers created economic and cultural impacts. For instance, the Great Appalachian Valley in eastern Pennsylvania provided a fertile area that drew many Germans who settled in great numbers and became the "Pennsylvania Dutch." They worked their way southward and soon occupied the Shenandoah Valley, partially opening a door to westward expansion by all the coastal-dwelling immigrants.

This led eventually to a conflict between the English and the French, since the movement through the few gaps in the Appalachians threatened the French trade empire of the interior. The resulting French and Indian War extended England's territory to the Mississippi River and its outcome was directly affected by the layout of the Appalachians. Concentrated along the coast for a century by this geological barrier, the English colonists were far more numerous and better supplied than the French, who had to rely heavily on their Indian allies. The Indians joined with the French largely because they understood the threat they faced if the English colonists ever breached the wall of the mountain range.

Millions of years of uplift, erosion, and renewed uplift by streams like this in the Appalachian Mountains created a layered barrier of mountains that shaped American history. *(USGS)*

After the war, the English sought to limit permanent settlements beyond the Appalachians by promulgating the Proclamation of 1763, which limited settlements of the original thirteen colonies to the area east of the Appalachians. The intention was to prevent further conflict with the French and their Indian allies. The result was to provoke resentment among the settlers in the British colonies, which contributed significantly to the later rebellion of the Revolutionary War. Thus, the complicated impact of a weary and eroded mountain range on the course of modern world history once again demonstrates the intimate connection between geology and history.

MOUNT MITCHELL AND ELISHA

That intimate connection between geology and history affects both nations and individuals, as evidenced by the strange, inspiring, and tragic story of the professor-explorer whose name is attached now to the highest peak of the Appalachians, Mount Mitchell. One of many nearly equal peaks in the Black Mountains section of the Appalachians, Mount Mitchell is covered with a deep forest. The peak is now not far off a highway,

---

THE APPALACHIANS'S MOUNTAIN-BUILDING PERIODS

Three major mountain-building periods assembled the Appalachians in the course of nearly 200 million years as the collision of continents first closed the Iapetus Ocean between North America, Europe, and Africa (Gondwana), then broke up the supercontinent of Pangaea:

+ **Taconic orogeny:** The first fit of mountain-building came 440 to 490 million years ago during the Ordovician period as continental collisions assembled the supercontinent Pangaea. Thrusting and folding in this period mainly affected the northern portion of the range. The 45-million-year Ordovician period ended with a major, global mass extinction that wiped out 60 percent of the species living in the ocean. Some scien-

The Smoky Mountains are part of the Appalachians and catch winter storms coming off the Atlantic, storing water in the form of snow, which is vital to the densely settled lowlands that surround the mountains. (*USGS*)

but for centuries it lay deep in the vastness of the mountains. The first white settlers did not begin to carve out homesteads on its flanks until the early 19th century, although various Indian groups have made use of its resources for perhaps 15,000 years. Early settlers found that range remote and forbidding, but with an abundance of wildlife. Mountain man Big Tom Wilson claimed to have killed 114 bears in the range in his lifetime. That profusion of wildlife on the slopes of the range eventually drew scientists as well, including botanist Elisha Mitchell (1793–1857). Working with the North Carolina Geologic Survey in 1825, Mitchell set out to explore and measure the range—including the then difficult task of determining which of the many peaks ranked as the highest.

Convinced that the unnamed peak in the midst of the Black Mountains was the highest point in the eastern United States, he headed into the wilderness in 1835 to make a series of measurements to settle the debate. He had to repeatedly climb every peak in the vicinity to make

tists have suggested that this extension might have been triggered by an intense gamma ray burst from the explosion of a neighboring star that wiped out the ozone layer and bathed the surface in radiation. Most scientists would argue that such mass extinctions stem from the intersection of a variety of factors, like climate change, volcanic activity, asteroid impacts, and invasive species.

+ **Acadian orogeny:** Between 400 and 350 million years ago during the *Devonian* period the Appalachians again rose, especially in the sections centered in New England and southern New York. During the Devonian period, the first fish evolved legs so they could venture onto the land, which had been largely without inhabitants. The first insects and spiders also moved onto the land. Meanwhile, the first seed-bearing plants spread across the once lifeless continents. Sharks and boney fish evolved in the oceans, where ammonite mollusks and trilobites dominated. The era ended with a mysterious mass extinction in which perhaps 75 percent of the marine species vanished. Some experts blame the extinction on the impact of an asteroid. Others suggest that the explosion of green plants relying on photosynthesis may have dramatically reduced the amount of *carbon dioxide* in the air, which could have produced a much colder climate. Evidence of widespread glaciers at the end of the Devonian supports this theory.

+ **Allegheny orogeny:** Uplift, folding, metamorphic transformation, and intrusions of granitic and volcanic rock some 300 million years ago as Pangaea began its breakup marked the final major period of mountain building in the Appalachians, this time affecting mostly the southern end of the range extending from Pennsylvania to Alabama. During this period, massive, swampy forests covered much of the area. Great layers of organic material in these swamps were the basis for the vital coal deposits of the range. Buried and compressed first into peat bogs, the organic carbons were eventually embedded so deeply that the heat and pressure fused them into coal, which is nearly pure carbon.

measurements. He could cover some 40 miles (64 km) in two or three days, climbing thousands of feet from the bottom of one valley to the next ridgeline. He often had to crawl on hands and knees on bear trails through thick stands of scratchy laurel. The trip up what is now Mount Mitchell required a trek of 18 miles (29 km) with an elevation gain of 3,800 feet (1,160 m). He emerged with measurements declaring the peak to be 6,480 feet (1,970 m) tall, making it the highest point measured in the United States up to that time. But his critics maintained that he either climbed the wrong peak or perhaps even faked the measurements.

Tragically, Mitchell's effort to defend his measurements would ultimately cost him his life. On another expedition in 1844, he incorrectly measured a different, nearby peak at 6,600 feet (2,000 m)—an error of several hundred feet. Based on his now mistaken measurement, Mount Gibbs was declared the nation's highest point. However, Geologist Thomas Clingman in 1855 measured both Mount Gibbs and Mount Mitchell more precisely and discovered Mount Mitchell was actually higher. In the world of scientific bragging rights, this would enable him to claim credit for discovering the highest peak. Mitchell, then 62, determined to return to the top of Mount Mitchell to reestablish his claim. On June 27, 1857, on his final visit to the mountain that would bear his name, Mitchell slipped and fell from a ledge above a 20-foot (6-m) waterfall. He struck his head and drowned in a deep, cold pool. Mitchell had apparently gotten lost in the thick underbrush on his way down. His body was found days later by tracker Big Tim Wilson, who followed his traces back down off the ridge. Several years later, the highest mountain in the Appalachians was named for Mitchell, when a U.S. Geological Survey expedition validated his original measurements. They also attached his name to the fatal waterfall. In the decades to come, the mountain he had explored at such cost would change dramatically. In the early 1900s, timber companies descended on the thick, old growth forests and cut down almost every tree in an astonishing space of 20 years. Today, the mountain is preserved as part of a national park and the peak lies not far off Interstate 40.

3

The Alps

Europe

The great Carthaginian general Hannibal in 218 B.C.E. stood staring at the massive barrier of the jagged, ice-capped peaks of the Alps, weighing whether he could battle both geography and the Roman armies seeking to trap him here against the seemingly fatal wall of rock. Around him, he had gathered 38,000 soldiers, 8,000 horsemen, and 37 armored war elephants. Ahead lay a frightening wilderness of 14,000-foot (4,270-m) high peaks, most sheathed in great glaciers, gleaming brilliant white in the thin air. Innumerable rivers thundering with ice melt blocked his path, snows covered the grass that might sustain his horses and elephants, hostile tribes haunted the passes, and the freezing cold waited to debilitate his soldiers. But the Roman armies were closing in on him here on the great plains of Europe, hoping to bring him to bay and make him fight far from the vulnerable heart of their youthful empire. Meanwhile, the lush, rich provinces of Rome lay safely behind that mountain range, protected on every other side from invasion by the great Roman navy.

Hannibal's only chance for victory against the bitter rival of Carthage lay through those deadly Alpine passes. He gave the order to his army to move into the mountain and so commenced one of the most famous military maneuvers in history. Fewer than half of his soldiers and only a handful of his elephants would emerge from those unforgiving mountains. But he fell upon the stunned Romans like a thunderbolt, using surprise and brilliant tactics to win a series of major battles. Even so, the Alps remained at his back, cutting him off from reinforcements and resupply from Carthage, far away in North Africa. In the end, even though he defied the mountain range, geography proved decisive—as it has so often proved in the intricate skirmishes, gambles, and disasters of human history.

In a real sense, the great wall of the Alps running across central Europe has shaped European history, and so the human history of the planet. The mountains protected Rome, which took advantage of its maritime dominance of the Mediterranean to lay the foundations of

Western civilization. Rome finally fell when warlike people to the north made it past the fortress of the Alps into Italy. So this jagged upthrust of rock shaped the whole history of the continent. (See upper color insert on page C-2.)

ALPS REVEAL DEEP SECRETS

In more recent centuries the Alps have also revealed the deep secrets of the Earth. Quite aside from offering the challenge that led to the invention of mountaineering in the 1800s, the Alps have become perhaps the best-studied mountain range on the planet. The Alps boast more than 50 peaks higher than 14,000 feet (4,270 m), the tallest of which is Mont Blanc, at 15,770 feet (4,810 m). The range stretches from Austria and Slovenia in the east, through Italy, Switzerland, Liechtenstein, and Germany to France in the west. Geologists have unraveled the deepest mysteries of the Earth by studying the intricate folds of ancient seabeds, great masses of fused and remelted rock thrust up from miles beneath the surface, and the bewildering jumble of rocks with dramatically different histories. The rocks of the peaks include pieces of oceanic crust, rocks from the deep *mantle*, and bits of crunched, buried and resurrected continents. This generations-long scientific effort to understand the complex layers and *cataclysms* of the Alps has made vital contributions to the understanding of the evolution of the Earth and the development of the theory of plate tectonics.

The Alps owe their complicated existence to a head-on collision between two great crustal plates—one carrying Europe and Asia, the other carrying Africa. Just to complicate matters, the sediments of a small ocean covering an oceanic crustal plate got caught in between. This three-way collision created a slow-motion cataclysm and the complex geology of the modern Alps. The ultimate rise of the Alps started more than 250 million years ago as the supercontinent of Pangaea began its inexorable breakup. Currents deep in the molten core of the Earth transmitted outward to the molten and semimolten mantle and then along to the crust caused the constant shifting of the crustal plates. The lighter, thicker, continental crust floated atop the dense rock of the plates, like icebergs. The great convection currents of the mantle forced the overlying plates to constantly bump up against one another, dragging the high-riding continents along with them. These crustal plates are constantly created anew along the great system of undersea fractures that cause a global network of undersea mountain chains, like the Mid-Atlantic Ridge. But since the surface of the Earth does not get any larger, the creation of new plate material at one edge demands the destruction beneath the great *undersea trenches* of a similar amount of material at the other end. So the plates move like conveyor belts, carrying the floating bits of continents along.

Sometimes, the lighter rocks of the continents are pulled down into the trenches, but more often they get scraped off the descending plate. That scraping process has built most of the great mountain chains, like the Alps, the Himalayas, and the Andes. It also accounts for why rocks on the continents are often 1 or 2 billion years old, while the oldest oceanic crust is merely 200 to 300 million years old. The oceanic crust is constantly created and consumed—endlessly recycled. But the light crustal rock floats along, surviving the destruction of one plate to be scraped off and carried away by a new plate.

Studies suggest a certain pattern in all this crustal plate destruction and continental movement. Evidence suggests that about once every 500 million years, this movement winds up smashing together most of the light continental rock. So instead of having seven scattered continents, during such periods a single great continent accounts for most of the land area. In fact, projections of continental movements suggest that we are currently about halfway through one of those cycles and that the continents will reconvene in another 250 million years or so.

So the roots of the Alps go back to the last time the continents gathered together in the supercontinent geologists have dubbed Pangaea, which was formed from the merger of two earlier massive continental masses—Gondwana and *Laurasia*. This great continent spanned the equator of a planet without ice caps, a land of vast inland seas, mild temperatures, great interior deserts, and limitless marshes. It proved the perfect setting of a great proliferation of life, including the rise of the dinosaurs and other life-forms.

The earlier collision between Gondwana and Laurasia had raised a great chain of mountains. In such a collision, sometimes the plate edges buckle and fold, raising up great piles of rock from each continent. Sometimes, one crustal plate rides up over the other, scraping rock off the top of the *subduct*ing plate but driving the smaller, over-ridden plate deep down into the mantle. The descending plate begins to melt miles beneath the surface. Geologists have named the great mountain chain raised by that first collision the Hercynic range. Once Gondwana and Laurasia were fused into Pangaea and the crustal plate motions shifted, the Hercynic range stopped rising and started eroding. Its fused, metamorphic rocks were reduced to gravel and sand and washed down into the lowlands, where they would eventually be reconstituted to become the distinctive sandstones and conglomerates of the later Alps. So these surviving rocks in the current Alps bear witness to the entire birth and death of an older mountain range. Moreover, the shallow seas that covered much of the area during this period resulted in the formation of great layers of limestone in the seabeds. Made from the skeletons of tiny creatures that died and settled to the bottom of these shallow seas, limestone is one of

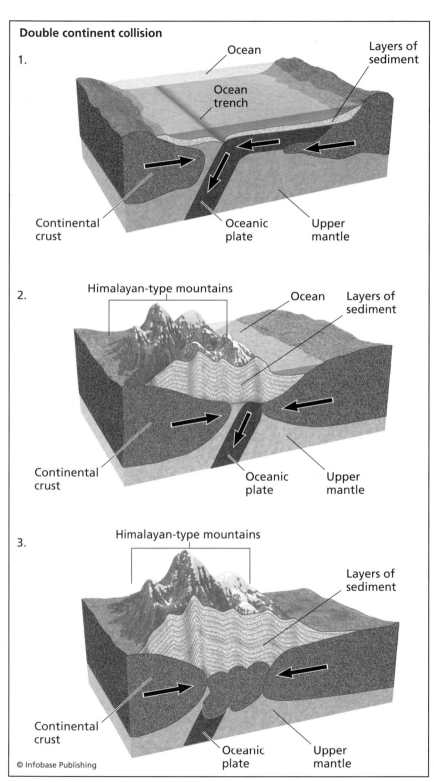

Double continent collision

1.

Ocean

Layers of sediment

Ocean trench

Continental crust

Oceanic plate

Upper mantle

2.

Himalayan-type mountains

Ocean

Layers of sediment

Continental crust

Oceanic plate

Upper mantle

3.

Himalayan-type mountains

Layers of sediment

Continental crust

Oceanic plate

Upper mantle

© Infobase Publishing

Mountain building

the most revealing of rocks. The steady rain of these calcium-rich remains formed layers that compressed under their own accumulating weight to eventually form limestone. Such thick, level limestone layers mark the one-time existence of an ocean bottom, even when eventually lifted to the top of Mount Everest or the lofty peaks of the Alps.

Some 180 million years ago at the start of the *Jurassic* period, the crustal plates once again shifted in their movements. At that time, the oceans brimmed with fish, squid, ammonites and great sea-going dinosaurs like the Ichthysaurs and the long-necked Plesiosaurs. On the land, the giant plant-eating dinosaurs were harassed by the small ancestors of the great meat-eating dinosaurs, and the ungainly, batlike Pterosaurs dominated the skies. During the 70-million-year-long Jurassic period, marshes bordered by gigantic ferns and palmlike cyads began accumulating the organic sediment that would eventually be buried, pressurized, heated, and turned into the oil and coal deposits that sustain modern economies. The Jurassic period actually draws its name from the Jura Mountains on the edge of the Alps between France and Switzerland, where much of the study of modern geology had its start.

At the onset of the Jurassic, a narrow new ocean began to open up along a *fissure* that began to split open Pangaea. As a result, what would become North America, Europe, and Asia moved north while the future Africa and South America moved south. The dense oceanic crust fused from the magma that forced its way to the surface along this rift system formed a growing mass of oceanic crust labeled the Piemont-Liguria Ocean, an arm of the much larger Tethys Ocean further east. Because no continental landmasses existed near the North or South Poles in the Jurassic, the planet lacked ice caps and sea levels were much higher. Shallow seas connected these ocean basins where limestone continued to form. The Piemont-Liguria Ocean never grew as large as the Atlantic Ocean, which also began forming in this period. Instead, it was more like today's Red Sea, a narrow rift between continents.

BREAKING UP IS HARD TO DO

During the *Cretaceous* period, plate movements once again shifted. During this heyday of the dinosaurs that ended some 65 million years ago, Pangaea shattered and scattered and the continents moved to approximately their present location. The Atlantic Ocean opened up and Europe and Africa began to move back towards one another. As they moved, they squeezed the small Piemont-Liguria Ocean between them. South America, Antarctica, and Australia went rifting away from Africa as the South Atlantic and Indian Oceans formed. The Tethys Sea narrowed towards its own extinction, since limestone pieces of its bottom sediments would eventually end up stranded atop Mount Everest after a head-on continental collision raised the Himalayas. In the chunk of continental crust that would become North America, broad seas separated the ranges ancestral to the Appalachians and the Rocky Mountains. In the area that became India, some shift deep beneath the surface resulted in an outpouring of lava that created the Deccan Traps, the largest recorded outflow of lava known. Despite the geological instability, the Earth remained warm and tropical during most of this period. The vast, shallow inland seas so effectively buffered the climate that tropical plants flourished at latitudes now beset by snow and glaciers. The mild climate and vast landmasses allowed the dinosaurs to flourish and diversify. Flowering plants emerged and spread across the surface, laying the foundation for a great diversification of other species—especially insects. Ants, termites, grasshoppers, and aphids developed into their present forms. Birds and mammals began to evolve and diversify, always in the shadow of the dinosaurs. The Cretaceous ended with a mass extinction that remains the topic of debate. The dinosaurs and most other living species vanished in a relatively brief period. Many scientists blame the effects of a giant asteroid that smashed into the Earth near the present-day Yucátan Peninsula. Such an impact could have raised a planet-wide haze of smoke and dust that blocked the Sun's rays causing a deep freeze that lasted for decades. Others suggest that such an impact may have simply administered the final blow following widespread climatic changes and tectonic and volcanic activity that made most species vulnerable to the asteroid's impact.

Many of the most important rocks that eventually comprised the Alps date to this period. As the continents changed gears and moved towards one another, the soft marine sediments of the small ocean basin that had briefly separated them were compressed and folded. The seafloor between Africa and Eurasia was squeezed and then forced down under the newly fragmented Apulian plate. Africa rode up over the leading edge of the smaller plate for perhaps 600 miles (970 km), pushing its leading edge deep down into the upper reaches of the semimolten mantle. The collision not only forced the leading edge of the Apulian plate deep into the Earth, it folded and compressed the upper layers. This initially created a long chain of island arcs in the trapped and dwindling ocean. Japan and the Aleutian Islands today form a similar arc of volcanic islands along the edge of a subducting plate. The volcanic rocks made from this melted, buried crustal rock remain prominent in the Alps today.

By the end of the Cretaceous, the ocean between Europe and Africa had vanished, subducted or compressed into great folds geologists call nappes. Now without the low-lying ocean basin to consume, the two continents staged a head-on shoving match as the Apulian subplate collided with Europe. Now the formation of the modern mountains began as the two continental masses met in a great pileup. Before, the low, dense oceanic plate could dive down under the overriding continental plate. But when two equally light masses of rock came into contact, the collision caused uplift, folding, and the rearing of up a great mountain chain. While the colliding continents jammed into one another, the tremendous weight and continued movement of each of the colliding plates also put tremendous pressure on the buried oceanic plate to continue descending. With the leading edge of the subducted plate some 45 miles (70 km) beneath the surface, great blobs of rock melted, recrystalized, and oozed back up towards the surface. These great buried masses of reforged, dense rock would eventually make their way up from great depths to form some of the most distinctive features of the modern Alps.

At some point, much of the connection between this still descending mass of crust and the lighter rocks of the mountains was largely broken by the accumulation of pressure. This allowed the continental crust that had not yet been pulled beneath the surface to bob upwards, freed from the drag of the descending crust. The developing mountains rebounded upwards—rising faster than they might have otherwise. Geologists have invoked the same explanation for the even more rapid rise of the Andes in South America. The process continues today in the Alps, although the continued rise of the mountains is largely balanced by ongoing erosion. The continued collision and uplift raises the height of the Alps by up to about half an inch (1.3 cm) per year.

HYPEREROSION SETS IN

The Alps were further shaped by a remarkable event that took place some 6 million years ago. The mountains underwent a period of dramatically increased erosion that clawed thousands of feet off their tops at a rate perhaps 10 times as great as the present rate of erosion, according to a study by researchers from the University of Washington. This surprising phase was directly connected to changes in the nearby Mediterranean Sea, which demonstrates the intimate connection between mountains and the surrounding terrain.

The Mediterranean separates Europe and Africa, a 965,000-square-mile (2.5 million km²) ocean basin, connected to the Atlantic Ocean by the nine-mile-wide (14-km) Strait of Gibraltar. It averages 4,500 feet (1,390 m) in depth, and totals some 29,000 miles (46,000 km) of coastline. Western civilization grew up on its shores, in large measure because the warm, relatively storm-free sea provided easy connections for trade and culture between early civilizations. This spawned a rich cross-fertilization of ideas and commerce. Geologists once thought the Mediterranean was a fragment of the ancient Tethys Ocean that separated Africa and Europe. However, more recent studies suggest that the two continents collided and then separated, leaving a gap when the crust beneath the Mediterranean Sea dropped. The sea first formed in the late *Triassic* and early Jurassic as a result of this dance of the plates.

Some 2 million years ago, further shifts in the crust closed off the Mediterranean's connection to the Atlantic. Now a vast, salty lake with no connection to the sea, the Mediterranean eventually evaporated. This left massive salt flats some two or three miles below sea level. Known as the Messinian Salinity Crisis, this event had a dramatic impact on the Alps, which then probably rivaled Mount Everest in height.

Suddenly, the streams cutting into the Alps had a descent of an extra two or three miles (3 or 5 km), which enormously increased their erosive power. The steepness of a river's watershed makes an enormous difference in its cutting power. For instance, the Mississippi River drains a much larger area than the Colorado River and carries far more water. However, the Colorado River is one of the steepest major rivers in the world. This explains why the Mississippi meanders over a great, flat floodplain and the Colorado has cut the Grand Canyon in the space of perhaps 5 million years. The drying up of the Mediterranean gave the rivers draining off the Alps the gradient of the Colorado River. As a result, the rate of erosion off the tops of the Alps increased more than tenfold, according to recent estimates. This period of rapid erosion continued for the next 3 million years. That extended high erosion rate probably also reflected a climate shift that produced much more rainfall, according to the results of the study by a team led by Sean Willett, a University of Washington geologist. The team charted earthquake faults now deeply buried and studied rock types. They concluded that the Alps once extended far down into Italy, reaching as far south as Milan. The period of hypererosion probably narrowed the Alps by about 120 miles (190 km) and eroded 1,000 to 5,000 feet (300–1,520 m) off the highest summits.

GLACIERS APPLY FINISHING TOUCH

The next major shift to shape the Alps after this period of increased erosion was a succession of glacier-spawning ice ages that in the past 2 million years put the finishing touches on the current spectacular landscape of the Alps. Five major ice ages have shaped the terrain, each one spawning a massive expansion of glaciers that often reached depths of 3,000 feet (910 m). Such glaciers advance and retreat as the climate shifts, carrying along massive loads of rock and debris that scour the rocks beneath them. Glaciers grind through rock so efficiently, that they create broad, U-shaped valleys with steep sides, rather than the V-shaped valleys cut by rivers. Glaciers half a mile (.8 km) thick rampaged out of major valleys and advanced 60 miles (100 km), chewing up everything in their path before retreating when the climate shifted and the ice age eased. Climate experts still do not fully understand why these tremendous planetwide cold spells occurred periodically over a 2-million-year span up until about 10,000 years ago. Most suspect some variation in the Sun's output perhaps synchronized with small variations in the Earth's orbit and tilt towards the Sun.

The most recent ice age ended 10,000 years ago. Evidence suggests that the glaciers that had advanced out of the Alps down onto the low-lying areas retreated abruptly with the warming of the planet, melting and moving back up into the mountains in a geological blink of an eye of 200 to 300 years. The glaciers left behind a twisted, churned up landscape, with great walls of debris where the glaciers dropped their accumulated loads as they melted back from the leading edge. Gigantic boulders now sit on mild hillsides, many miles from their origins, having been carried along by the advance of the glacier.

The glaciers of the Alps have resumed their retreat after 10,000 years of stability. One recent study by scientists from the University of Zurich predicted that the Alps could lose 80 percent of their glaciers by the end of the 21st century as a result of a projected average global temperature rise of about 5°F (3°C). Overall, the glaciers of the Alps have been shrinking for the past 150 years, although the speed of the meltdown has increased markedly in recent decades. In the 1970s, the 5,150 Alpine glaciers covered 1,120 square miles (2,900 km²), which even then represented a 35 percent decline from the extent of the glaciers in the 1850s. Currently, the loss from the 1850s ice cover has reached about 50 percent. If current trends continue, by the end of the century only a handful of small glaciers on the highest, coldest peaks will survive, the scientists estimated.

The loss of glaciers worldwide has important effects both locally and globally. Locally, glaciers are often vital in regulating the water supply of people hundreds of miles away down in the valleys where rivers, streams, and springs are all fed by the gradual melting of glaciers throughout the year. During ice ages, glaciers gain more ice in the winter than they lose in the summer and the glaciers grow. For most of the past 10,000 years, the glaciers in the Alps have been mostly in balance—adding ice in the winter and melting a little in the summer, providing reliable water to the valleys below in the warm months. Now, many of the plants, animals, and human beings who depend on the glaciers may have to make painful adjustments as the great masses of ice up in the mountains dwindle.

Moreover, water draining off glaciers worldwide as the planet warms could raise sea levels significantly, according to estimates by scientists from the University of Colorado at Boulder. Perhaps half of the estimated 650 billion tons of ice that melt into the oceans each year comes from small glaciers and ice caps. Each year, these mountain glaciers and ice caps add to the ocean enough water to fill Lake Erie. As the glacial melt accelerates, the current .12 inch (.30 cm) average annual rise in sea level will increase, totaling perhaps several feet by the end of this century. Such a global rise in sea level could create serious problems for many coastal cities, including low-lying areas like the U.S. Gulf Coast, San Francisco, and heavily populated areas such as India and Bangladesh.

The retreat of the glaciers worldwide has spurred climate experts to predict a crisis in providing enough fresh water. In fact, the Rocky Mountains, Andes, and several other major mountain ranges could lose half of their snow pack as a result of climate shifts caused by the current global warming trend, according to a study by the Pacific Northwest National Laboratory. The study predicted that snow pack losses by 2100 would total 61 percent in Alaska, 61 percent in the Alps, 56 percent in Scandinavia, 57 percent in the Rocky Mountains and Cascades, and 45 percent in the Andes.

HANNIBAL SUCCUMBS TO GEOGRAPHY

Of course, Hannibal probably would have appreciated less snow and fewer glaciers in his history-shaping crossing of the Alps. Although historians still debate his route, military histories credit it as one of the great marches in ancient warfare. After struggling through the snows and across the glacial rivers of the high Alps, he emerged in northern Italy in the economic center of the Roman domains. He then fought a brilliant series of battles, in which he outmaneuvered and destroyed numerically superior Roman armies. In the Battle of Lake Trasimene, he crossed marshes and the Apennines, offshoots of the Alps, to take a Roman army by surprise. He marched skillfully around his enemies flank and trapped the Romans in a narrow space against a lake.

In the spring of 216 B.C.E., Hannibal won his most dramatic victory at Cannae in northern Italy. He cut off an unwieldy joint Roman army of some 100,000 soldiers from their source of supplies to the south. The over-eager Roman generals charged at Hannibal's army, hoping to smash the Carthaginians by weight of their superior numbers. Instead, Hannibal allowed the center of his line to fall back while the rest of the line stretched around to encircle the seemingly victorious Romans. Hannibal then sent in his cavalry and shifted to the attack, so that the Romans found themselves under attack from the sides and rear. This tactic devastated the Roman system of interlocking of forward-facing shields and spears on which traditional warfare was based at that time. In the ensuing carnage, up to 70,000 Romans were killed and captured, including nearly a third of the Roman senators and half of Rome's top military commanders. By contrast, Hannibal's outnumbered army suffered only light losses. The battle proved the most catastrophic defeat in Roman history and one of the greatest single-day casualty tolls in the history of warfare.

Even so, the Alps would not let Hannibal have his victory. After Cannae, the Romans largely kept their distance and Hannibal found himself trying to supply an army in the field by seizing the crops of local farmers. Carthage could send him no reinforcements due to the presence of the Roman navy and the still imposing barrier of the Alps. Although Hannibal sustained himself in northern Italy for years, his force was gradually worn away. Carthage eventually negotiated an end to the war. Hannibal himself fled when the Romans demanded his surrender. He served as a military adviser to various other enemies of Rome, but ultimately killed himself when his then host agreed to turn him over to the Romans. In the end, the great barrier of the Alps shaped the course of Western civilization, just as they continue to shape the climate of Europe and the evolution of the planet's surface.

Mid-Atlantic Ridge

North Atlantic

The Earth's greatest mountain range is hidden and its oddest but most important peak is all but ignored. But this hidden range and this fuming, belching mountain have done more to shape the history of the planet than any other feature on the globe. The Mid-Atlantic Ridge runs for some 42,000 miles (67,600 km), but most of its fierce, jagged peaks never come to within a mile (1.6 km) of the sunlight. The ridge does break into the open air in one place—the bizarre volcanic island of Iceland, with its frequent eruptions, geothermal energy, icy climate, and unusual human history. Even though few people have ever seen or visited the Mid-Atlantic Ridge, its emergence has determined the position of most of the continents on Earth. The titanic forces that have built the Mid-Atlantic Ridge in barely 200 million years have also repositioned every continent and shaped all of human history.

The Mid-Atlantic Ridge forms a great crack in the Earth's thin, brittle crust of rocks. It winds nearly from pole to pole, a chain of loosely connected volcanic mountains. The most prominent mid-Atlantic section runs for 12,000 miles (19,300 km), with a width of 600 to 2,500 miles (970–4,000 km). This means that the hidden, raw volcanic terrain of the Mid-Atlantic Ridge actually covers a startling one-quarter of Earth's surface, almost all of it deep beneath the surface of the ocean.

MID-ATLANTIC RIDGE VALIDATES THEORY

The discovery of the Mid-Atlantic Ridge was one of the defining events in the development of the theory of plate tectonics, which revolutionized scientific understanding of the Earth. The discovery and mapping of this underwater mountain chain ultimately validated the theory of continental drift, first proposed by Alfred Wegener in the early 1900s. Wegener's theory was an attempt to explain the strange match between the rock layers and fossils of widely separated mountain chains, like the Appalachian Mountains in North America and the Atlas Mountains in North

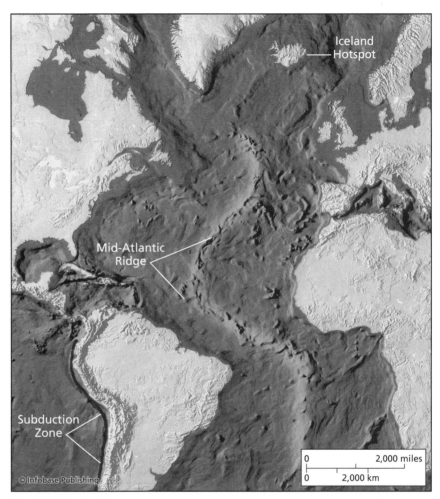

The Mid-Atlantic Ridge

Africa. Wegener proposed that all the continents had once been gathered into a single supercontinent dubbed Pangaea, but that they had some how broken apart and "drifted" to their current position. Since he could not explain how whole continents could "drift," few geologists took his theory seriously.

However, the discovery of the extent of the Mid-Atlantic Ridge dramatically changed the terms of the debate. Prior to the mapping of the Mid-Atlantic Ridge, many geologists believed that the differential cooling of the different types of rocks largely accounted for the rise of mountains and the opening of deep rifts. As field geologists meticulously measured the rock layers contorted on the surface, this theory of mountain building through planetary cooling began to fall apart. For instance, the folded-up rock layers in the Appalachians and Alps were comprised of hundreds of miles of crunched and folded layers, far too much folding to stem from any plausible contraction related to the cooling of the Earth.

Moreover, surveyors like George Everest uncovered a fresh problem for the cooling Earth theory when they provided measurements of the world's highest peaks. These early surveyors used instruments to precisely measure the density of the rock making up the mountains. But they soon discovered that the sheer mass of the mountains all around them had enough gravity to affect the measurement. To calculate the height of the mountains, they had to account for the effect of the mass of the surrounding mountains on their instruments. When they tried to introduce this fudge factor, they were surprised to find that huge mountains like Mount Everest had only about half the mass they expected. They concluded that the mountains themselves were composed of light rock with deep roots. That means the light rocks of the mountains were effectively "floating" like an iceberg on top of dense rock beneath. That surprising finding conflicted with the idea of a uniform, shrinking Earth. Geologists also discovered that many rocks have natural *radioactivity*. This gradual decay of elements in the rocks generates heat and that internal heat would prevent the Earth from cooling fast enough to wrinkle up into mountain ranges and ocean basins.

This revelation prompted many geologists to reconsider Wegener's discarded theory of continental drift. Perhaps the continents could be moved as a result of something happening down in the molten and semi-molten layers beneath the hard, brittle crust. Maybe the heat of the radioactive rocks could melt the crust, so continents could slide along on top, as a thick slab of glass can flow without ever actually becoming liquid. Other clues emerged from the seafloor itself. Scientists had long assumed that the bottom of the deep ocean was a flat plain, buried beneath eons of mud, too cold, deep, and lightless to sustain life. Early attempts to find the bottom with cannonballs on ropes and cables only demonstrated the miles-deep extent of the oceans. However, some soundings in mid-ocean detected undersea mountains, including an intriguing chain of underwater peaks in the middle of the Atlantic Ocean.

The first effort to systematically explore the world's oceans on a scientific basis dates back to the epic, three-year voyage of the HMS *Challenger* in 1872, which circled the globe and measured the depth every 100 miles (160 km) with a 200-pound (90-kg) weight on a line connected to a hand-operated winch. The first hints of a strange mountain range in the middle of the Atlantic Ocean came in the mid-1800s when American Lt. Matthew Fontaine Maury set out to make as many measurements as possible and combine them with hundreds of soundings by U.S. Navy vessels and fishermen. This first crude contour map of the Atlantic Ocean revealed a shadowy mountain range miles beneath the surface. Maury called it "Middle Ground" or "Dolphin Rise."

Explorations of the ocean floor made a gigantic leap in the 1920s when the U.S. Navy began to experiment with making crude depth maps by bouncing pulses of sound off the seafloor, then waiting for the echoes to return to the ship. By calculating the travel time of the signal, scientists

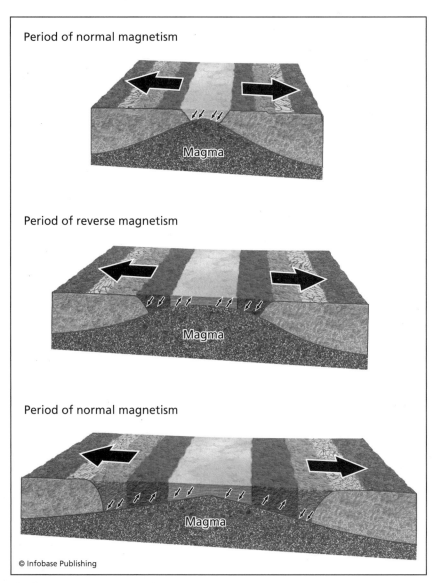

Period of normal magnetism

Magma

Period of reverse magnetism

Magma

Period of normal magnetism

Magma

© Infobase Publishing

The formation of an ocean ridge

could finally get a rough measurement of the depth of the ocean across wide swaths. Other scientists developed instruments that could directly measure the force of gravity. Once they figured out how to tow those instruments along behind ships, they discovered strange decreases in gravity readings in the ocean.

These overlapping measurements prompted some scientists to dust off theories of wandering continents to see if they could think of some physical force that would move the continents about. University of California professor David Griggs made a model of the Earth using a tank full of oil to represent the deep, fluid layers of molten rock. He covered the oil with a thin film of wax, to represent the hard, solid crust of the Earth. Then he used rotating barrels to create convection currents, similar to the roiling boil of a pan of water. Sure enough, the slow *convection* currents in the oil moved the paraffin layers. Perhaps currents in the semimolten deep Earth could in the same way move the thin, brittle rock of the crust.

Next, Griggs studied measurements of hundreds of earthquakes gathered by earthquake experts Beno Gutenberg and Charles Richter. The earthquakes were caused when two gigantic slabs of rock suddenly slipped past each other, with the break often starting many miles beneath the surface. Griggs seized on this work to suggest that perhaps the earthquakes were caused by movements of the rock down at the boundary between the crust and the mantle where these deep convection currents hit the hard, brittle rock of the crust.

Vital confirmation for the theory of continental drift came finally as a result of scientific advances forced by World War II. After Adolf Hitler in 1939 unleashed his stunning blitzkrieg and conquered much of Europe with shocking ease, England found itself an island under siege. Britain's survival now depended on a lifeline of supplies from the United States, which Hitler soon sought to sever with submarine attacks on Britain's vital convoys. This prompted the U.S. Navy to pour money into anything that might help ships navigate across the deep ocean and enable their destroyer escorts to locate and sink lurking submarines. Research money now supported a handful of scientific labs that specialized in the study of the ocean, including Woods Hole Oceanographic Institution in Massachusetts, Scripps Institution of Oceanography in California, and Lamont Geological Observatory at Columbia University. These three great research laboratories would ultimately lead to one of history's great scientific revolutions.

The navy immediately began probing the ocean with sonar sound waves, hoping to get an echo off a hidden submarine. Several scientific breakthroughs led to the development of instruments that could use sound waves to map the deep seafloor. These detailed maps made navigation across the Atlantic for the convoys and their protectors far easier. The large-scale mapping efforts soon revealed mysterious, flat-topped mountains rising from the Atlantic plain. Scientists decided these were former volcanic islands that had been drowned by the rising sea level, their tops flattened by wave action. The seamounts, or *guyots*, provided excellent navigational markers for ships crossing the ocean, but they also posed a new mystery for geologists. Many of these flat-topped peaks remained thousands of feet beneath the surface. Scientists did not understand how they got there and how they could have ever been close enough to the surface for waves to flatten their tops. Not even the most frigid of ice ages could have lowered sea level so far.

The new sonar maps soon revealed a stunning view of the seafloor. The single most striking feature was the most spectacular geological feature on the Earth, the 12,000-mile-long (19,300-km) Mid-Atlantic Ridge, which is four times longer than the Andes, Rocky Mountains, and Himalayas combined. Its shape echoes the outlines of North and South America, Europe, and Africa. The steep, jagged zone of mountains rearing upward from the seafloor averages about 500 miles (800 km) in width, with many peaks rising 20,000 feet (6,100 m) from the seafloor. Along much of its length, a narrow, mile-deep (1.6 km) rift valley snakes along the crest. Moreover, thousands of massive of east-west running canyons and ridges offset the north-south running Mid-Atlantic Ridge. To add to the mystery, research ships dragging iron dredges across the ridge brought up raw chunks of young volcanic *basalt*. Clearly, the seafloor was not a great, broad plain, but a young, dynamic, violent landscape.

Unfortunately, much of the data gathered by the navy during the war remained highly classified, so scientists Bruce Heezen and Marie Tharp converted the specific measurements into an exquisite map of the seafloor, using color-coded shadings to exaggerate the vertical relief but leaving out the classified actual depths. The stunning image, released in the 1950s, transformed geologists' view of the seafloor. The map shows the massive Mid-Atlantic Ridge, which breaks the surface at volcanic Iceland. Clearly, the scientists mapping the ocean bottom had discovered a new and unexpected world. Geologists would have to abandon the notion of the flat, buried seafloor and explain a world every bit as dynamic, surprising, and active as the continents.

WORLD'S GREATEST MOUNTAIN CHAIN

The high point of the Mid-Atlantic Ridge is Iceland, a strange, fuming, geologically bizarre island in the North Atlantic. Iceland is built from the outpourings of innumerable *volcano*es, much like those miles beneath the ocean's surface that built the Mid-Atlantic Ridge over the past 200 million years. The world's most volcanically active piece of ground, Iceland is bigger than the state of Georgia and rises from the ocean halfway between ice-buried Greenland and frigid Scandinavia at the northern tip of Europe. Steam rises routinely from hundreds of cracks in the Earth and a dozen volcanoes sputter and smoke. During the last Ice Age 12,000 years ago, the scrap of land and the fuming volcanoes were all hidden under layers of ice miles thick. The ancient Greeks had gathered hints of the remarkable island of steam and fire, which Phyheas of Massalia in 300 B.C.E. described as an island at the edge of the world six days north of Britain.

In the eighth century, a band of Irish monks set out in boats made of animal skins stretched over twigs to seek God on that semilegendary land. They became the first settlers, living among the volcanoes and geysers. A century later the Vikings established the first permanent colonies on the island. From here, Eric the Red set out to discover Greenland, after he was exiled from Iceland for killing a man. Icelanders also discovered North America, long before Columbus. Leif Eriksson, nicknamed Leif the Lucky, reached North America in 1000 C.E., before returning to Iceland. Columbus would not happen on the continent for another 500 years.

But settling Iceland proved a difficult process, thanks in part to the fury of the volcanoes that built it in the first place. The early settlers lived uneasily with the threat of cataclysm. In 935 C.E., a 20-mile (32-km)-long rift opened up on the island and out spewed 20 cubic miles (83 km³) of lava in the course of eight years. The constant eruptions spurred a rich mythology among the stubborn Icelanders. They tell the tale of a magician who turned himself into a whale and swam to Iceland, where he found it already inhabited by a fierce clan of creatures made of fire and ice. The Icelanders nurtured stories that populated the restless, angry, and capricious land with trolls and fairies and sprites, spirits of the Earth and the ocean expressed in the hot springs and outbursts of molten rock.

The population endured outbreaks of disease, crop failures, and famines in the course of their centuries-long occupation. One massive, three-year eruption in 1783 started at Mount Lakagigar and created a rift some 15 miles (24 km) long. Instead of the normal, slow-moving wall of lava released by most Iceland volcanoes, this time the lava poured out accompanied by a strange blue smoke. Even in far-off Europe, people turned to the west to note the blue-tinted sky. The gas contained great billows of sulfur dioxide that proved poisonous as a rain of ash settled all over the island.

The series of eruptions produced the greatest outpouring of lava in recorded human history. Other much larger eruptions have taken place in the distant past, like a flood of lava 65 million years ago that covered

660,000 square miles (1.7 million km²) in India. But this was the largest flow ever actually witnessed. The eruption proved disastrous for the Icelanders. Some three cubic miles of rock gushed up out of the earth, covering 224 square miles (580 km²) and adding new land to the island. Moreover, the poison sulfur dioxide settled into the soil and killed most of the plants. The livestock soon starved, which led to famine among the Icelanders. Isolated from the rest of the world, one third of the population starved in the next two years. The explosion offered a devastating object lesson in the dangers of living on a mid-ocean ridge. Geologists have been struggling for decades to understand the geologic forces that created Iceland in the past 20 million years. The island spews lava at a crooked elbow where the mostly north-south Mid-Atlantic Ridge turns to splinter into a complicated ridge system on the floor of the Arctic Ocean.

Geologists are not sure why the ridge breaks the surface so dramatically to form Iceland, while most of the peaks of the planetary ridge system remain more than a mile (1.6 km) beneath the ocean's surface. One leading theory suggests that Iceland sits above the sort of geological *hot spot* that built Hawaii, a stationary weak point in the crust where molten rock from the *mantle* heats overlying rock and causes a permanent volcanic zone. Perhaps the evolving rift that created the Mid-Atlantic Ridge essentially fractured the crust and hit the existing hot spot, which would explain why so much more molten rock has flowed to the surface here than elsewhere along the ridge structure. Some geologists point to the great mass of Greenland to support the theory, suggesting that as the crust shifted the hot spot that had previously built Greenland moved to the current location of Iceland along the ridge zone. Here, the existing fractures in the crust lock the wandering hot spot into place.

If that theory is true, then the hot spot that first built Greenland started causing eruptions some 130 million years ago. The rift spread north until about 60 million years ago when it split Scandinavia from Greenland and began opening up the Arctic Ocean. At that point, the hot spot that would eventually create Iceland was beneath Greenland, according to conventional theory. Of course, geologists still debate the nature and cause of such geological hot spots as Hawaii and Yellowstone. Once, most experts believed that hot spots probably started as a result of some weakness in the crust that allowed a bubble of molten mantle rock to melt the underside of the crust and reach the surface. This theory suggests that the superheated, molten rock in the hot spot plume rises like a hot air balloon through the earth. In that case, a hot spot would resemble a lava lamp, in which a blob of heated, less dense oil rises in slow motion through surrounding, cooler oil. The Iceland hot spot could have created

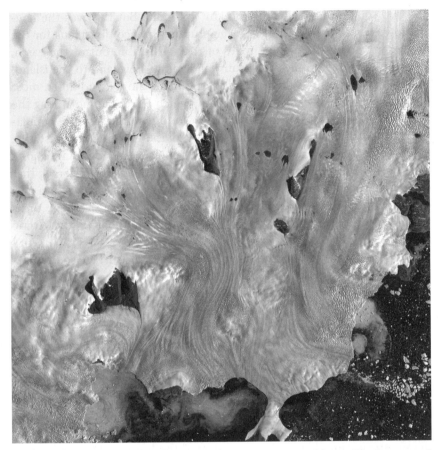

A great ice sheet once connected Greenland, shown here in this satellite image, and Iceland, the most dramatic outcropping of the planet-girdling Mid-Atlantic Ridge. Pictured here is Greenland's western coast and a small field of glaciers surrounding Baffin Bay. *(NASA and USGS)*

a 1,240-mile (2,000-km)-wide plume of molten rock that finally reached the surface.

ICELAND CONFIRMS HOT SPOT THEORY

Iceland has already helped confirm the theory that hot spots are driven by this rising balloon of less dense, molten rock. Recently, Georgia Institute of Technology researchers used a supercomputer to model the movement of molten rock between 18 and 1,700 miles (29 and 2,720 km) beneath the surface. The calculations were based on measurements of the speed of waves of energy generated by earthquakes. Such seismic waves move faster in solid rock than in molten or semimolten rock, so a change in the speed of these seismic waves offers information about the interior of the

Earth. Seismic waves spread out in all directions from the epicenter of an earthquake, so measuring seismic wave arrival times at different monitoring stations reveals information about the density and temperature of the rock on the path between the epicenter and the measuring station.

The *geophysicists* hoped that this complicated calculation would reveal the size and temperature of the plume of molten rock under Iceland. The measurements did reveal a great plume of less dense rock rising from at least 60 miles (100 km) beneath Iceland, which meant it started out in the upper layers of the mantle. The plume boosted the temperature in the surrounding rocks just enough to drive the volcanoes of Iceland. However, geophysicists do not know for sure what actually drives these hot spot plumes. Some experts speculate that perhaps the plumes originate in the melted leading edge of a plate that has been *subduct*ed. The molten rock then finds its way back to the surface along *fissures* in the overlying crust of the uppermost plate.

Other geophysicists suspect the answer lies deeper, in the upper reaches of the mantle, where massive currents drive the movement of crustal plates. Some 1,700 miles (2,720 km) below the surface, the molten core of the Earth meets the semisolid rocks of the mantle. Convection currents in the core cause related currents in the mantle, which in turn press up against the 15-mile-thick (24-km) crust. In perhaps 40 known places, this creates a stable hot spot like Iceland, say some experts. Geologists have determined that these hot spots do wander slowly, but at only a fraction of the speed of crustal plates.

As the Atlantic Ocean opened up, Greenland began drifting northeast over what would eventually become the Iceland hot spot, according to this theory. The idea got a big boost from seafloor mapping that showed undersea mountains running from the coast of Greenland straight to Iceland. This submerged Aegir Ridge suggests Iceland was created by a stationary hot spot that got locked into place when it hit the fractures in the crust along the Atlantic Ridge. Geologists estimate the Aegir Ridge stopped growing 25 million years ago, just before Iceland began to rise from the ocean.

On the other hand, several scientists argue that the lava that continually resurfaces on Iceland really comes from a piece of the Earth's crust that melted on the leading edge of a subducted plate, not from a hot spot connected directly to the mantle. Scientists from the University of Durham and the Geological Survey of Norway base that unconventional conclusion on the way magnetic stripes on the seafloor line up. The alignment of the magnetic elements in the seafloor *magma* can be dated by using the known timing of magnetic pole reversals. Therefore, these magnetic stripes help geologists reconstruct the movement of the continents and the evolution of the ridge system. The magnetic patterns on the seafloor between Greenland and Iceland are much more confusing than the orderly stripes on each side of the Mid-Atlantic Ridge. In fact, the patterns cast doubt on whether a hot spot could have moved from Greenland to Iceland in the past 50 million years. Moreover, critics of the dominant theory that Iceland was formed from the intersection of a hot spot and a ridge system insist that a hot spot could not have produced nearly enough lava to build the landmasses in the area.

In a fascinating illustration of how science works, advocates of the hot spot plume theory have fought back with alternative explanations. Perhaps there were multiple plumes, muddling up the picture. Perhaps, instead of a single plume, there was a long rift, which allowed hot mantle rock to bubble up along a line instead of in a single spot. Perhaps the superheated hot spot magma hit fractures spreading outward from the ridge and extended out through a network of cracks to reach the surface. The critics of the conventional hot spot theory eventually proposed a completely new explanation. They suggest that the rift that broke up Pangaea created the Mid-Atlantic Ridge as it spread north towards the area of Greenland and Iceland. Here, three different crustal plates collided. In the pile-up, the smallest plate was forced down far beneath the surface. Eventually, the solid rocks melted. That would mean the magma that built Iceland would come from melted down crustal rocks, rather than deep rocks from the mantle. The difference in chemistry between light continental crust and deeper rock could account for the perplexing amount of lava that reaches the surface around Iceland. Moreover, a huge slab of melted, upwelling crust could generate a lot more lava on the surface than a single, narrow plume that had to blowtorch its way up through the mantle, they argued. Geologists are still battling out the contrasting theories, knowing that finding the truth in Iceland may hold the key to understanding the entire, complex system of ridges, trenches, hot spots, and contending crustal plates.

THE PEOPLE OF MOUNT HEKLA

In the meantime, Icelanders live in a geologist's dream and a farmer's nightmare. Iceland now gets more of its energy from geothermal sources than any nation on Earth, thanks to the island's abundant geysers and hot springs. This helps Icelanders withstand the long, harsh winters. The steaming landscape remains so populated by myth that it is the only place on the planet where the government routes roadways to avoid the traditional dwelling places of trolls and fairies. Perhaps a belief in spirits and myth flows naturally from living precariously on an ice-shrouded island with 24 active volcanoes.

Mount Hekla erupts about once every five years, coughing smoke and spitting ash to the delight of the hardy geo-tourists. The very word "geyser" comes from the name of an explosive spring of hot water in Iceland that has since largely subsided. On the island, great rifts run for miles, punctuated by volcanoes and V-shaped cracks that march along twisting paths. Desolate *plateaus* of jagged lava support strange sorts of moss, but remain too rough and jagged to walk across. One 150-foot (46-m) waterfall spilling over the edge of a sheer wall of lava generates a continuous glimmer of rainbows. The government at one time wanted to build a dam above the waterfall to generate electricity, but abandoned the idea when a young woman threatened to throw herself over the falls if the government built it.

The combination of fire and ice has created other dramatic effects. Some 8,000 years ago, the whole island was buried under a layer of ice several miles deep. This mass of permanent ice actually connected Greenland and Iceland. The volcanoes continued to send molten rock steaming up against the bottoms of this vast ice sheet, creating lakes inside the ice cap. When especially violent eruptions melted all the way through to the surface above these lakes, it could release a titanic flood. As the Ice Age waned and many of the glaciers retreated, these glacial floods gouged out the land, leaving the dramatic steep valleys and deep fjords leading out to sea. (See lower color insert on page C-2.) Such ice lakes still exist, since permanent glaciers currently cover about 10 percent of the Iceland. The largest Icelandic glacier, Vatnajökull, covers 3,000 square miles (7,770 km²) with a layer of ice up to half a mile (.80 km) thick. (See upper color insert on page C-3.) You could easily hide every single glacier in Europe in this single mass of Icelandic ice.

Meanwhile, the Icelanders continue to demonstrate their adaptability as they thrive on their little piece of the Mid-Atlantic Ridge. Most heat their homes with steam and run their appliances with electricity generated by steam turbines built atop the vents. Between 1963 and 1966, a whole new island rose out of the ocean as a result of the eruption of an underwater volcano. The newly forged Surtsey is one of 15 fresh little islands fed from the same blob of underground magma that drives the volcano Hekla. Some biologists think that these islands mark the opening of a new spreading center parallel to the existing plate boundary some 60 miles (100 km) west, the seed from which new oceans may grow.

VOLCANO THREATENS TOWN

A completely new volcano erupted on January 22, 1973. Iceland's latest mountain was dubbed Eldfell. Black ash and lava poured out of the central crater, rolling down on the town of Heimaey and towards the narrow-necked harbor on which the fishing village utterly depended. As the crater emptied, the mountain collapsed, sending a slow-moving wall of molten rock rolling towards the heart of town. The 5,000 residents fled as the wall of lava consumed houses on the outskirts of town. Firemen rushed to bring to bear fire hoses, hoping to cool and harden the advancing lava and create a wall that would divert the lava into the ocean. Miraculously, they stopped the lava about one-fifth of the way through town, saving most of the buildings. But as the lava flowed into the ocean, the townspeople realized that it could easily block the narrow harbor entrance on which the economy of the village depended. So the firemen shifted their lines and again doused the leading edge of the lava. Remarkably, they once again stopped the lava. In the end, the flow of rock out into the ocean actually improved the existing harbor by creating a new natural breakwater.

5

The Sierra Nevada

California, the Western United States

Everything had gone wrong. But the infamous Donner Party of 87 immigrants seeking a new life in California did not know just how disastrously wrong their struggle across the continent had gone until the snow began falling in a deluge of fluffy flakes high in the imposing Sierra Nevada in October 1846. Already worn by their months-long effort to get their wagons, oxen, and families across the immigrant trail to the promised land of California, they made camp just short of a mountain pass that led through the great wall of granite to wait out the unexpectedly early heavy snowstorm. Camped in a dramatic uplift of granite that had originally hardened into a great blob of rock miles beneath the surface on the edge of a complex boundary between two crustal plates, the men, women, and children of the Donner Party hoped to wait out the storm and finish their journey. What they did not know was that the early blizzard signaled one of the most severe winters in decades in a mountain range whose peaks included the highest spot in the lower 48 states. They also did not know that a trapped winter of starvation would kill half of them and spur perhaps the most famous episode of cannibalism in the nation's history.

A SERIES OF UNFORTUNATE EVENTS

The families that set out from Independence, Missouri, in early May 1846 had little conception of the fatal mountain range that lay near the end of their journey. The main group included the families of George Donner and his brother Jacob, James Reed and his family, and various hired hands for all three families—about 33 people. After a week of travel, they joined a large wagon train under the leadership of William H. Russell, who traveled with them for the next two months along the California Trail. Worried about their late start and slow progress, they decided to take a shortcut called "Hastings Cutoff." The group of 87 who wanted to take the shortcut broke off from the main wagon train in Wyoming and elected George Donner as their leader.

On July 31 they set off on what would prove a lethal journey that took them on a poorly developed trail through the Wasatch Mountains and the Great Salt Lake Desert. The route eventually rejoined the California Trail near present-day Elko, Nevada, but they had lost a vital three weeks, putting them in the Sierra Nevada just in time for the snowstorm that trapped them high on the mountain.

They camped in two groups at what is now called Donner Lake and Alder Creek. They soon ate their oxen, but that did not sustain 87 people for very long. By mid-December, they faced near-certain starvation. A group of 15 men resolved to brave the deep snows high on the mountain and set out on snowshoes to seek help at Sutter's Fort, some 100 miles (160 km) distant on the far side of the mountain range. As they struggled through the renewed snowstorm, one man gave out and they left him behind. But soon a blizzard trapped the whole party. Four more men froze to death as they huddled together, trying to wait out the storm. Starving now, the survivors ate the bodies of their dead companions. When the storm abated, they struggled on. When three more men died of exhaustion, the others ate their bodies as well. Seven men finally made it through the mountains on January 18, 1847, to bring word of the trapped women and children deep in the Sierras.

People in California organized a total of four rescue parties, which attempted to reach the still-trapped and starving main body of the Donner Party. The first group of rescuers reached the party's camp in February, to find that 14 people had died. The survivors had subsisted on boiled ox hide and scraps of plants and food, but had not resorted to cannibalism. The first rescue party on February 22 set out with 21 survivors who were strong enough to travel. The second rescue party arrived a week later and discovered that some of the 31 people left behind had started to eat the dead, although the extent of cannibalism remains controversial. Recent studies of remains and bone fragments have concluded that perhaps the widely reported cannibalism was actually quite limited. The study of thousands of bone fragments conducted by researchers from the University of Oregon and the University of Montana concluded that at most one group of 12 people resorted to cannibalism in the last few weeks they were trapped before the arrival of the later rescue missions. The second relief expedition rescued another 17 survivors. The third and fourth relief efforts found only one survivor and brought him out to Sutter's Fort on April 29. All told, 41 immigrants died there on the mountain and 47 survived.

The lurid publicity given to the Donner Party made the high peaks of the Sierra Nevada infamous throughout the world. The mountain range formed the final barrier to the rush of thousands of people to California, a stream that became a flood when prospectors discovered gold nuggets in the sands of Sutter's Creek just two years after the Donner ordeal.

Although the mountains earned their fame as a result of the barrier they posed to travel, they have since fascinated geologists as a result of the tale the rocks tell of the construction of the North American continent from bits and pieces gathered up by the restless movement of crustal plates.

North Dome and Basket Dome in Yosemite National Park are examples of the massive granite formations formed from deeply buried plutons of molten rock that cooled and hardened deep beneath the surface before being uplifted and exposed by erosion. (F. C. Calkins, USGS)

The Sierras stretch for just 400 miles (640 km) along the eastern boundary of California and form the physical transition from the geologically pasted-together terrain of California and the sequence of mountain ranges of the interior west known as the Basin and Range Province. Running along a great system of faults, *rifts*, and fractures, the Sierras rise abruptly from the high desert vistas on the east side, but slope more gradually down into California's Central Valley on the west side. Rivers that flow off the western flank of the mountain have filled the Central Valley, providing the level terrain and deep soil to make it one of the most productive agricultural areas in the world. The rivers that drain the western flanks run eventually to the Pacific Ocean, although California's current elaborate system of dams and canals uses that snowmelt to help sustain about 10 percent of the nation's population. The streams that drain off the eastern flanks of the Sierras are trapped in the Basin and Range Province. Even here, the thirst of urban areas like fast-growing Los Angeles asserts itself. The drainage from the Sierras once fed the Owens River near present-day Bishop, California, but Los Angeles bought up thousand of acres of rich farmland to gain control of the water rights. The Los Angeles engineers diverted the water into a great aqueduct, leaving the Owens Valley a desert of swirling dust.

The Sierra Nevada contain a host of natural marvels, including the deep, shockingly blue waters of Lake Tahoe, the awe-inspiring granite forms of Yosemite National Park, groves of the most massive trees on the planet, dramatic glacially scoured valleys like Hetch Hetchy, Kings Canyon, and Kern Canyon, and the towering peaks of Mount Whitney, which at 14,500 feet (4,420 m) is the highest point above sea level in the United States outside of Alaska.

MOUNTAINS REVEAL CONTINENT'S HISTORY

The story of the mountains reveals much about the evolution of North America and presents one of the most complex and absorbing rock sequences on the continent. The story starts some 150 million years ago during the *Jurassic* period, just as the dinosaurs were rising to dominance. Most of the continents were then gathered into a single landmass. At that point, a great island arc chain like modern Hawaii or Japan was embedded in a crustal plate that collided with the uplifted continental rock floating atop the North American Plate. Such island arcs are generally formed by volcanoes fueled by the melting of a *subduct*ed plate. When this chain of volcanic islands collided with North America, it spurred the first episode in the creation of the Sierra Nevada known as the Nevadan *orogeny*. The collision heated, melted and reformed the rocks of the volcanic island chain, creating rocks that eventually became part of the current Sierra Nevada.

The rising heat and pressure in the depths of the Earth caused masses of this now buried crustal rock to melt into great blobs deep below the surface. These blobs of granite, called *plutons*, formed at various times between 115 million and 87 million years ago. Their chemical composition recorded their history as they slowly cooled and hardened into the great masses of granitic rock that give the Sierra Nevada their dramatic topography. Up above on the surface, erosion had worn the great mountain chain raised by the collision of crustal plates down to gently rolling hills by the time the dinosaurs died out 65 million years ago.

Some 25 million years ago, a shift in the movement of the plates triggered a new period of uplift and mountain building. The block of crust beneath the Sierra Nevada began to rise and tilt to the west, pushed upward and deformed as a result of the jostling of crustal plates. Eventually, that uplift brought to the surface the once deeply buried plutons of granite, hard, crystallized rock that resists erosion much more stubbornly than the sediments that once lay on top of them. These blobs of rock that formed deep beneath the surface are today known as the Sierra Nevada batholith. The mountains continue to rise today, driving both the shape of the mountains and the underlying volcanic forces. The fault lines in the Sierras generate major earthquakes and connect in complex ways to the massive *San Andreas Fault*. Moreover, the forces that created a volcano near the famous Mammoth Mountain ski area left a great *caldera* or collapsed *magma chamber* that remains volcanically active. Geologists have detected a mass of molten rock deep beneath the surface there and predict it could one day cause a catastrophic eruption on the east side of the range. Rivers and streams have clawed at the rising peaks, leaving behind the jagged splinters of granite and spires that mark the range today. Moreover, a succession of ice ages created massive glaciers that sculpted the mountain range—leaving behind its accumulation of dramatic U-shaped valleys with sheer sides rising for thousands of feet.

YOSEMITE: WONDERLAND OF GRANITE

Perhaps the most dramatic demonstration of the history of the range lies in Yosemite National Park, a landscape so awe-inspiring that it played a key role in launching the modern conservationist movement. Yosemite sits on the western slope in the central Sierras, a spectacular granite-walled valley that is barely 7 miles long (11 km) and one mile wide (1.6 km), with sheer granite walls that rise 3,000 to 4,000 feet (910–1,220 m) from a flat, lush valley floor adorned by meandering streams. (See lower color insert on page C-3.) The valley boasts some of the most bejeweled waterfalls in North America, including 2,430-foot (740-m) Yosemite Falls, 2,140-foot (650-m) Sentinel Falls, and the world-famous 620-foot (190-m) Bridalveil Falls.

Glaciers carved the flat-bottomed, cliff-sided Yosemite Valley, slicing away the granite masses so sharply that spectacular waterfalls now spill out into midair, like Yosemite Falls shown here. *(F. C. Calkins, USGS)*

Moreover, the narrow valley includes some of the most dramatic masses of rock in North America, famous worldwide among climbers. The formations are made from the plutons of granite that first melted at the descending edge of a buried crustal plate, then cooled, hardened and were uplifted once again to the surface. Formations like El Capitan, Half Dome, Cathedral Rocks, and Three Brothers form some of the planet's most celebrated scenery. (See upper color insert on page C-4.)

The raw materials for these great masses of granite date back to rocks laid down in Precambrian times at the edge of the North American continent. At that time, the area lay on a passive, inactive continental margin much like the East Coast of the United States today. Sediments eroded off the low-lying mountains settled on the floor of a shallow sea. Deposits of *limestone*, sandstone, and *shale* formed in the shallows, as the accumulating weight of thousands of feet of added sediment compressed the older layers. As these sedimentary layers were buried and compressed, the rising temperature transformed them into marble, quartzite, and slate. Traces of these rocks remain scattered throughout the valley.

However, much of the rock that now forms the core of the valley underwent additional, dramatic alterations as a result of a change in the movement of the crustal plates. Starting in the mid-Paleozoic and lasting through the early Mesozoic, two plates collided as the supercontinent that composed most of the land mass of the planet broke up and scattered. The violent continental breakup continued for millions of years until the infant North America separated from Europe and Africa in the middle of the *Triassic*. Many of the sediments that would ultimately form the rocks

Inclined joints determine the westward slope of the upper surface of the Three Brothers in Yosemite National Park. *(U.S. National Park Service, courtesy of USGS)*

of the valley were on the edge of a subducted plate. Most of that melting took place some 210 to 80 million years ago and formed buoyant plumes of molten rock, or diapirs, some six miles (10 km) beneath the surface.

This great melting and refusing miles beneath the surface largely shaped the rocks that dominate in the Sierra Nevada and Yosemite today. Deep beneath the surface, the cooling plutons of granite picked up veins of other minerals like gold and silver, which seeped into fissures in the hot buried rock. In Yosemite alone, geologists have identified by their chemical composition at least 50 distinct plutons, now forming massive outcrops at the surface.

Next came a period of uplift dubbed the Nevadan orogeny. It raised a mountain chain that probably towered at least 15,000 feet (4,570 m). Ice and water immediately set to work on these jagged peaks as the uplift slowed, turning the great peaks into rolling foothills by about 25 million years ago. Erosion removed miles of overlying rock, eventually exposing the plutons of granite that lay at the heart of the range—and of the current Yosemite Valley.

At this point, another period of dramatic uplift took place. A 5-million-year-long spasm of volcanic activity started about 20 million years ago. The eruptions brought great masses of volcanic rock to the surface. Lava covered thousands of square miles and dammed valleys and rivers. During this period, a titanic series of eruptions formed what is known today as the Long Valley Caldera near Mammoth. Its last major period of activity dates back just 700,000 years, when an eruption 25,000 times as massive as Mount Saint Helens blanketed much of the region with ash. Lava last reached the surface perhaps as recently as 600 years ago and the area beneath the now mostly buried caldera remains prone to earthquakes as a result of the movement of molten rock beneath the surface.

Some 10 million years ago, another shift in plate motions spurred the uplift of the current Sierra Nevada and Yosemite Valley. Shifts in the tilt of the mountains changed the directions of rock-cutting streams, so that drainages like the Merced River cut across older drainage systems. That explains why Yosemite has so many spectacular "hanging" waterfalls—older streams that empty out into thin air after the retilting of the range caused glaciers and streams to cut new valleys.

Of course, like most of the interesting topics in geology, the age of the Sierras remains a matter of debate. Most geologists who have studied the mountains would probably agree that they rose to their present height fairly recently—perhaps in the past 3 to 5 million years. However, Stanford geology professor C. Page Chamberlain argued in a study published in the journal *Science* that the mountains are actually much older—perhaps 50 million years. He based his conclusions on an ingenious attempt to measure ancient rainfall. Page maintains that the mountains reached their current elevation approximately 40 to 60 million years ago, although they also rose 1,000 to 2,000 feet (300–610 m) in a relatively short period some 3 million years ago.

The Stanford scientists came to their conclusion by looking for clues to rainfall millions of years ago. To do that, they started with ancient rock exposed by environmentally disastrous mining techniques used in the 1800s. Miners then used massive, pressurized sprays of water to strip soil away from whole hillsides, hoping to expose nuggets and veins of gold. This devastated many Sierra hillsides, streams, and rivers, but also exposed 50-million-year-old rocks formed from clay layers. The Stanford scientists analyzed these rocks, seeking clues to the altitude on the mountain at which the clays formed. Rainwater contains various forms of hydrogen, including an extra-heavy variety called deuterium. Generally, the heavy deuterium drops out of rain at lower elevations. Therefore, the ratio between regular hydrogen and deuterium provides a clue as to how high on the mountain the raindrops originally fell. Since the raindrops were ultimately bound into the clay, the scientists did some complex calculations and concluded that the mountains were nearly their present height when the clay layers formed 50 million years ago.

The deep history of these rocks also accounts for the dramatic landscape that formed when once-buried granite comes to the surface. At the surface, these great granite bubbles encountered dramatically lower pressures than when they were formed. The release of pressure and the prying fingers of erosion caused the domed plutons of granite to flake away

GLACIERS SUPPRESS VOLCANOES

The enormous weight of layers of ice thousands of feet thick may actually smother the outburst of volcanoes from molten rock miles beneath the surface of the Earth, according to a surprising study by geologist Allen Glazner from the University of North Carolina at Chapel Hill. Glazner calculated the number of volcanic explosions in the eastern Sierra Nevada over the course of a million years, based on the lava and ash deposits. He then compared the volcanic explosions to the ice age periods when massive glaciers filled many of the valleys of the Sierras. He discovered a strong connection: When the glaciers expanded and exerted their great weight on the Earth, the number of volcanic explosions dropped sharply. When the glaciers retreated, the volcanoes often started up. He speculated that perhaps the weight of sheets of ice half a mile (.8 km) thick put pressure on the rock layers beneath. This might have narrowed the fissures and cracks through which the magma miles beneath the surface could escape to create a volcano.

The study demonstrated the unexpectedly delicate connection between events at the surface and deep volcanic forces. It also raised yet another possible impact of the current gradual warming of the planet. Studies show that glaciers are retreating rapidly on mountains all over the planet. As those glaciers retreat, it could trigger a global increase in volcanic activity. Such a volcanic outburst could pump even more carbon dioxide into the atmosphere, causing a feedback loop that would melt glaciers even more rapidly.

in a process called exfoliation. This splintering of the rock along the arch of fractures in the pluton's original form caused the distinctive, rounded shapes of formations like Half Dome and El Capitan. The release of pressure from these deep fractures also partially accounts for the valley's dramatic cliffs and deep erosion. Vertical masses of rock split off from the rock walls, forming the clean sheer faces of the valley's sides.

ICE AGES SCULPT ROCKS

A sequence of ice ages in the past 3 million years put the final touches on the Sierra Nevada in general and on Yosemite in particular. Climate experts believe that small variations in the Earth's orbit and historical changes in the composition of the atmosphere cause periodic ice ages. A sequence of four major glacier periods left their deep marks on the Sierras and Yosemite. The coldest—the Sherwin Glacial Period—lasted for 300,000 years and ended about 1 million years ago. The glaciers of this period did much of the carving of the U-shaped Yosemite Valley. Glaciers reached depths of 4,000 feet (1,220 m) in some valleys, an inexorable mass of ice that could carry house-sized boulders and deeply etch the bedrock over which they passed. The glaciers would typically advance in the winter and retreat in the summer, scouring the rock as they moved down the slope. During warming periods, they would retreat far up the valley and when the cold returned they would bulldoze their way miles back down the valley. In the process, they scraped out the distinctive U-shaped valley and the sheer granite walls. The glaciers roughly sanded

Glacial erratic, or block of rock, transported by a glacier and left precariously balanced near Olmstead Point as the ice melted in Yosemite National Park *(USGS)*

the cliff walls, creating the steep drops and smooth faces of Yosemite's most famous formations. However, the glaciers generally did not rise all the way to the tops of the cliffs, which accounts for the survival of a host of bizarre and delicate rock formations high on the walls of the deep valley.

Ironically, a debate about the glaciers of Yosemite played a role in a vigorous geological debate that ultimately helped spawn the modern environmental movement.

Josiah Dwight Whitney, chief of the California Geological Survey, played a leading role in studying the geology of the Sierra Nevada, which is why his name is attached to the highest point in the lower 48 states. The eldest of 13 children, he was a respected geologist when appointed California's state geologist in 1860. He organized a team of scientists that included geologists, botanists, and fossil experts to survey the geography of the state. The legislature cut off funding before he could complete his massive study, but he published three thick volumes and wrote an influential book about Yosemite in 1869. Whitney also became a leading advocate for protecting the valley. But he also soon came into odd and bitter conflict with an even more passionate and effective advocate for the valley—John Muir, who founded the Sierra Club and the modern conservationist movement.

Born in Scotland, Muir was a pugnacious romantic who loved brawls and bird nests. He immigrated to the United States in 1849, took up botany, and, after a factory accident nearly blinded him, made his way to California in 1868. His encounter with Yosemite was like a religious experience, unleashing his eloquent passion on behalf of this vivid landscape. Although he also worked as a ferry operator, sheepherder, and broncobuster, his life's work lay in advocating for the protection of wilderness areas—especially Yosemite.

Muir came into conflict with Whitney when he concluded that only glaciers could have carved the sheer cliffs and deep, U-shaped valley of Yosemite. Whitney, a much more influential and conventionally trained geologist, argued that a cataclysmic sinking of the valley floor explained the soaring formations and 4,000-foot (1,220-m) cliffs. The two men waged a fierce scientific battle. Whitney called Muir an "ignoramus" and a "mere sheepherder." He also suppressed information in his landmark geological survey of the Sierras that would have supported a glacial reworking of the valley.

Despite his credentials, Whitney gradually lost the scientific debate. His credibility was damaged when he was asked to examine a curious, apparently ancient human skull supposedly found 130 feet (40 m) beneath the surface. Whitney pronounced the Calaveras Skull evidence that human beings had reached North America between 2 and 5 million years ago. As it turned out, the skull was a hoax and no undisputed evidence of human occupation of North America older than about 15,000 years has since been found, although some experts argue for dates as early as 40,000 years.

But while Whitney's influence dwindled, Muir's importance rose. He gathered evidence of Sierra glaciers and did field studies of the Giant Sequoias, the planet's most massive trees. He became friends with many leading figures of his day, including Ralph Waldo Emerson and Gifford Pinchot, who would become the first director of the U.S. Forest Service. Muir also convinced President Theodore Roosevelt to visit Yosemite in 1903 and then took the president camping in the backcountry. This experience helped convince Roosevelt to support making the area a national park in 1905.

HEARTBREAKING LOSS OF THE SECOND YOSEMITE

However, not even Muir's great influence was enough to save the nearby Hetch Hetchy Valley, which Muir called a "second Yosemite." The state built a dam across the Tuolumne River, which drowned the valley to create a reservoir. Muir lobbied fiercely to save the valley, even appealing directly to Roosevelt. However, he was no match for the big money lined up behind the reservoir. Although his tenacity engendered years of debate, President Woodrow Wilson finally approved construction of the dam. Devastated, John Muir died in 1914, of what his friends described as a "broken heart." But he left as his legacy the protection of Yosemite, passionate writings about the value of wild places, and the drive to create the Sierra Club and other conservationist organizations.

The Sierra Nevada have also played a role in history and in the climate and topography of the western United States. The steep, sharp-rising wall of rock forms a physical and ecological barrier between the warm, mild environs of California and the harsh, interior spaces of the Southwest. First, the mountains rise so sharply from the great, flat expanse of the Central Valley that they effectively catch most of the storms that brew up in the Pacific and blow inland. Such moisture-laden storms blow across California, hit the wall of the Sierra Nevada and must rise over the mountains. But as the warm wet air rises towards the 14,000-foot-tall (4,270-m) peaks, the air cools. The colder the air gets, the less moisture it can hold. As a result, most storms that hit the steep flanks of the Sierras drop their snow and rain on the mountain peaks. This has created the rain shadow desert of the Great Basin on the far side of the Sierras.

The rapid change in altitude along the Sierras has created a multitude of different habitats for plants and animals. The foothills of the mountains include great expanses of scrub and chaparral varieties, with few trees and high desert winters. But the plant and animal communities

LAKE TAHOE WARMING UP

The effects of global warming may already be having a big impact on one of the world's most beautiful lakes, the startling blue Lake Tahoe high in the Sierra Nevada. Tahoe's 1,650-foot (500-m) depth is second only to the much smaller Crater Lake in the Cascade Mountains of Oregon. Tahoe is 22 miles (35 km) long and 12 miles (19 km) wide, with a surface area of 191 square miles (495 km²). The lake's basin formed when the mountains on either side rose, and the block of crust beneath the lake dropped between 2 and 3 million years ago. Glaciers then scoured the basin deeper about a million years ago. Snowmelt soon filled the great gouge in the earth until the waters rose high enough to drain out at the top down the Truckee River.

Like the rest of the Sierra, the ground beneath Lake Tahoe remains active and often surprising. One recent study by University of Nevada at Reno researchers reported a cluster of 1,600 small earthquakes centered 20 miles (32 km) beneath Lake Tahoe. The researchers connected the flurry of deep quakes with an 8-millimeter uplift of the land beneath Tahoe. The researchers said the earthquake swarm and the uplift reflected a three-foot (1-m) rise in a great mass of molten rock 20 miles (32 km) below the surface.

Native people lived on Tahoe's shores for thousands of years, but the first nonnatives to see it were Lieutenant John C. Fremont and his guide Kit Carson. They happened upon the lake in their trailblazing exploration of the Sierras in 1844—a few years ahead of the ill-fated Donner Party. The lake derives its startling blue color from its deep, nutrient-starved waters, which don't have enough minerals to allow the growth of *algae* that give many lakes a greenish cast. Once famous for the visibility of its clear waters, the lake has become a recreational mecca and has started to suffer the consequences. Drainage from the developments around the lake has introduced nitrogen and phosphorus, which have fueled the growth of algae—resulting in a decline in visibility. Moreover, according to recent studies, the temperature of the water has started to rise at a rate of 0.027°F (−17.76°C) per year since 1969, spurring a further growth in algae.

change steadily with the elevation, from shrub, to foothill woodlands, to low pine forests, to sub-alpine forests, and finally to the treeless, frozen alpine zone above 9,500 feet (2,900 m). The mountain range boasts some 1,300 different unique plant species, but a full 10 percent of them are now endangered—thanks largely to human activities and the introduction of exotic species. Perhaps the most distinctive and impressive of the range's plant species is the giant sequoia, the planet's most massive plant. One of three species of redwoods, the giant sequoias reach an average height of 150 to 280 feet (46–85 m) and an average diameter of 16 to 23 feet (5 to 7 m). Record trees have grown to 300 feet (90 m) high, 30 feet (9 m) in diameter, and reached ages of up to 3,200 years.

However, they have been affected by the changes inflicted by human beings—especially as a result of the century-long effort to control wildfires. The sequoia's life cycle is intimately connected to wildfires. The trees attain their massive girth in part because of a two-foot-thick sheath of bark. This protects the tender, water-carrying tissues of the trunk from the effects of fire. The giant trees need periodic wildfires to clear out the competing, smaller trees and underbrush, and to prepare the soil to nurture the seeds of the redwoods. In fact, the sequoia's pine cones generally only open and spread their seeds after they are damaged by fire. Although the trees do not produce any cones at all until they are at least 12 years old, they can then produce stupendous quantities. A single mature tree may disperse 300,000 to 400,000 seeds per year in some 11,000 cones.

Even though only a handful of the hundreds of millions of seeds produced in the long lifetime of a single tree need root and survive for the trees to thrive and spread, they have been undergoing a long decline. That probably reflects the impact of fire suppression and livestock grazing in the early and mid-20th century. This effort for decades prevented the low intensity ground fires to which the sequoias had adapted. Instead, the dead wood on the forest floor and smaller trees built up to such densities that when fires did finally escape control, the flames scorched the roots or climbed up to the tops of the thickets of smaller trees and into the lower branches of the giants.

Forest managers finally recognized the impact of eliminating natural fires in the 1970s and have since tried to reintroduce controlled fires. That effort is complicated by the great buildup in fuel loads as a result of the previous fire control policy. Biologists hope the trees will recover and resume reproducing effectively. However, change comes slowly for trees that have been growing for 3,000 years. The plight of the sequoias and the now uphill efforts to protect and restore them stands as a meta-

Rain shadow desert

phor for the problems facing many of the natural systems in the Sierras, from the native frog species that were nearly exterminated when people planted trout in high Sierra lakes to the host of native plants and animals threatened by introduced species.

One of the most dramatic human impacts may prove to be the gradual warming of the planet that many climate experts attribute to the pollution-spurred buildup of *greenhouse gases*. One recent study predicted that the gradual warming of the planet will result in a 70 percent decline in the Sierra's snowpack in the next 50 years, a change that could have a dramatic effect on plants and animals and human beings that depend on the slow, predictable spring water supply from melting snow on the distant peaks.

Ironically, the model predicts that rainfall in the mountain range might actually increase. But the rain will likely come during the warmer months of the year instead of during the big winter storms that deposit the great mounds of snow on the upper peaks that doomed the Donner Party in the 1800s. So the shift in climate and rainfall patterns may generate more destructive floods storming out of the mountains, but less spring and summer runoff. That could dry up streams and severely affect the cities, towns, farms, and wildlife living in the drainage area of the great mountain range.

Forecaster L. Ruby Leung from the Department of Energy assumed that the concentration of greenhouse gases in the atmosphere will continue to increase at a rate of about 1 percent per year. That will spur an estimated 1.5 to 2 degree centigrade increase in average temperatures through the middle of the 21st century. As a result, the snowline in the Sierras will probably rise from 3,000 to 4,000 feet (910 to 1,220 m), resulting in a 70 percent decline in the average annual snowpack. Already, the researchers noted, the Coast Ranges to the west have lost an estimated 60 percent of their snowpack due to the warming of the past 50 years. That might have saved the Donner Party, but it could mean trouble for the plants, animals, and people of the modern Sierras.

6

The Andes

South America

The Andes form a jagged, lofty wall along the west coast of South America, the world's longest above-water mountain chain. The mountains account for the greatest elevation change in the world, a 40,000-foot (12,200-m) plunge from the top of its tallest mountain to the bottom of an undersea trench just offshore. Since its formation between 138 and 65 million years ago, the range has shaped the climate of a continent, revealed deep mysteries about the structure of the Earth, and once sustained one of the world's most adaptable and interesting ancient civilizations.

The range includes 50 peaks higher than 20,000 feet (6,100 m) and an overall average height of 13,000 feet (4,000 m), second only to the Himalayas. Aconcagua, its highest peak, rises to a breathtaking 22,840 feet (6,960 m). Although not as high as the peaks of the Himalayas, the Andes rise straight up from sea level, while the Himalayas are perched on a high plateau in central Asia. Moreover, the Andes rank as the world's longest chain, stretching for nearly 5,000 miles (8,000 km) from the coast of the Caribbean Sea in the north to the island of Tierra del Fuego in the south. The outriders of the Andes run through seven countries—Venezuela, Colombia, Ecuador, Peru, Bolivia, Chile, and Argentina.

THE ANDES'S STRANGEST LAKE

The Andes harbor one of the world's strangest lakes, the huge Lake Titicaca, which is the highest commercially navigable lake in the world. Gleaming in the thin air at 12,510 feet (3,810 m) above sea level on the border of Peru and Boliva, the lake gathers the flow of 25 rivers. Although the lake has an average depth of 280 feet (85 m), it also has 41 islands, many of which support large human populations. Meltwater from glaciers on the surrounding mountains largely sustains the lake. The Desaguadero River flows out of Lake Titicaca to the south, but that accounts for only about 5 percent of the water the lake loses every year. Most of the water that flows into the lake simply evaporates, vanishing into the thin, dry air.

For most of its astonishing length, the Andes is composed of two parallel mountain ranges, with a deep valley in between. Probably named for the *Quechua* word "anti," the Andes offer one of the most vivid and revealing examples of the effects of plate tectonics—the force that ultimately lies beneath the construction of most of the planet's great mountain chains.

ABRUPT RISE POSES MYSTERY

Geologists have struggled to account for the abrupt rise of the Andes, especially so close to the deep Atacama Trench that lies just 100 miles (160 km) offshore and runs along the coast of Chile and Peru for some 3,670 miles (5,870 km). That makes it the longest undersea trench on the planet, shadowing the longest chain of mountains. Plunging to a depth

Steep-sided volcanic cones in the Andes Mountains along the Chilean-Argentinean border add texture to this satellite image produced by NASA. Of approximately 1,800 volcanoes scattered across this region, 28 are active, but uplift and volcanic outpours make the Andes the fastest-rising major mountain chain on the planet. *(NASA and USGS)*

of up to 26,460 feet (8,150 m), the 40-mile-wide (64-km) trench covers an area of 228,000 square miles (590,520 km²).

The comparatively young mountains continue to rise at a dramatic speed, perhaps the fastest such uplift on the planet. The speed of the uplift clearly has everything to do with the collision of great crustal plates, which also accounts for the presence of the deep, seafloor trench that parallels the mountain range. Just off the western coast of South America the *East Pacific Rise* splits the seafloor as a result of *magma* welling up into this great fracture in the Earth's crust. This pressure from below is splitting the giant Pacific Plate from the much smaller Nazca Plate to the east. This relentless pressure along the fissure drives the Nazca Plate against the South American Plate to the east at a speed greater than any other plate boundary on the planet—about seven inches per year. The Atacama Trench formed where the small, dense, 3.8-mile-thick (6-km) Nazca Plate plunges underneath the lighter, 25-mile-thick (40-km) South American Plate. This titanic collision both created the trench and raised up the Andes—partly through uplift and partly through volcanism. As the Nazca Plate was forced down beneath the thicker, lighter South American Plate, the heat and pressure rose with each increase in depth. Eventually, the leading edge of the descending Nazca Plate melted and the highly pressurized, molten rock combined with water and other elements and expanded upward through a network of *fissures*. This fueled a chain of volcanoes that created great stretches of the tall, jagged Andes Mountains. The process also triggered frequent earthquakes, with epicenters that pinpoint the depths at which the buried Nazca Plate is breaking up.

The process started some 200 million years ago as the supercontinent Pangaea was splintering and fragmenting and the Atlantic Ocean began to open. That is why the oldest rocks in the Andes are a relatively youthful 250 to 450 million years old and most are much younger volcanic rocks. The Andes now has the world's tallest volcanoes, although most remain so remote from human settlements that they cause relatively little damage.

The mountain range consists of two jagged, parallel ridges separated by a long valley, which provides almost the only farmable land in the whole, rugged country. For hundreds of years, this high valley sustained the complex civilization of the Incas, whose brilliant and sophisticated farming methods supported a larger population than lives in the area today. But despite the complexity of those crustal plate collisions, geologists have still had trouble accounting for the sheer speed of the rise in the mountains. Leading theories suggest that the Andes may offer clues to what is happening much deeper beneath the surface. The explanation for the speed of the mountains' rise may lie at the still poorly understood boundary between the light, brittle rocks of the crust and the dense,

MYSTERY LINKED TO THE MANTLE

The rocky shell of the Earth's mantle makes up 70 percent of the total volume of the planet. Above the 1,800-mile-thick (2,900-km) mantle lies the thin continental and oceanic crust made of the lighter rock that cooled and solidified at the surface. *Geophysicists* have mapped and studied the mantle which starts three to 50 miles (5–80 km) miles beneath the crust. The key measuring tools are the seismic waves produced by earthquakes, which pass from the solid crust into the semimolten mantle. A distinct boundary layer called the Mohorovicic Discontinuity—or Moho—defines the upper reaches of the mantle. Here, the seismic waves abruptly change speed. Geophysists believe convection currents in the mantle drive the movement of crustal plates at the surface and suspect those currents are in turn connected to movement in the molten, iron-rich, superdense core of the planet. The upper reaches of the mantle are relatively cool and chemically distinct from the great bulk of the rock much deeper in the mantle. This brittle and chemically different layer of both mantle and crust is called the *lithosphere*, which extends to a depth of about 60 miles (100 km) from the surface.

Below that lithosphere lies the asthenosphere, a relatively plastic layer of the mantle that lies about 155 miles (250 km) beneath the surface. Here, seismic waves slow down markedly, indicating a change in the temperature and composition of the rock. Mantle temperatures range between 930°F and 1,650°F (500°C and 900°C) near the bottom of the crust and as high as 7,200°F (3,980°C) deep down near the solid core. Although most of the rock of the mantle is technically solid, the intense pressure and heat causes the rocks to move in a slow, viscous deformation. This sets up a massive convection current in the mantle, in which hot rock rises like the blob of heated oil rising in a lava lamp. The rise of this heated material spurs a corresponding descent of cooler rock from closer to the surface. These great cells of rising and falling material create the fractures of the crustal plates, feed energy into volcanoes, and ultimately cause the rise of mountain chains like the Andes.

semimolten rocks of the earth's mantle layer. For instance, distinctive elements in the lava produced by some volcanoes in the Andes suggests that the cracks and fissures beneath the mountain range may go all the way down to the *mantle*. (See lower color insert on page C-4.)

One line of evidence involves gases escaping from volcanic vents. Geologists have tested gas samples from volcanic vents in the Andes and discovered traces of helium that probably came directly from the Earth's mantle. The distinctive form of helium found in the volcanic vents had to have come from deep beneath the surface, suggesting a connection with the mantle.

Other researchers have found additional links between the accelerated rise of the mountains and the Earth's mantle miles beneath the surface. Researchers from the University of Rochester concluded that the mountains have actually risen twice as fast as many geologists believed—more than half a mile (.80 km) per million years. They based the still-controversial estimate on a complex analysis of sedimentary *carbonate* rocks that have formed in the past 5–12 million years. These carbonate rocks form in a chemical reaction with water. The researchers realized that this reaction could give them an idea as to the elevation at which those carbonate rocks originally formed. That is because rain high on a mountaintop has different ratios of certain types of oxygen than rain that falls at lower elevations. Therefore, they had a way to estimate at what altitude the carbonate rocks formed. The scientists then compared the elevation at which the rocks formed to the elevation at which they were found. The resulting estimate of the breakneck speed of the mountains' rise has spurred much debate among geologists.

This dramatic landscape has built a wall of rock along the whole of South America's west coast, which has had an intense impact on the

The rain shadow effect of the towering Andes Mountains has created the Atacama Desert, one of the driest places on Earth. In this view, the desert meets the foothills of the Andes in a tangle of salt pans and gorges choked with mineral-streaked sediments that give way to white-capped volcanoes. *(NASA and USGS)*

climate and on the human beings who have lived here for thousands of years. The climate in these great mountains varies all along the length of the range, depending on elevation, the presence of the ocean, and ocean currents. In the south, it is rainy and cool. In the center, it is dry and cold—with one great desert so trapped between surrounding walls of mountains that it goes for years at a time without rain. This region was so high and cold and dry that it was used to test robot rovers designed for use on Mars. In the north, the mountains are rainy and cold, with a tropical rainforest sprouting at the foot of glacier-covered peaks. But all along its length, the Andes largely control the temperature and rainfall throughout the region. By forcing moist ocean air to rise over the great barrier, the Andes determine the distribution of deserts, rain forests, and farmland all along their length.

THE INCA BUILD A COMPLEX CIVILIZATION

Despite the hardships imposed by the jagged, remote landscape of these mountains, the Andes once sheltered one of the world's most distinctive and well-adapted civilizations—the Inca. Building on the cultural foundations of earlier, lesser-known people, the Inca established the largest empire in the Americas prior to the arrival of the Spanish. The Incas first emerged from the high *plateaus* among the Andes in Peru in about 1197. In the next 400 years, they used a shrewd combination of conquest, bribery, and peaceful assimilation to spread their organization and culture throughout the central Andes. They brought most of western South America under their sway, including much of modern Ecuador, Peru, Bolivia, Argentina, and Chile. Although the people under their control spoke at least 700 different languages, the Inca's Quechua language unified the sprawling empire. Divided into four regions that each had a ruler and a bureaucracy, the Inca Empire was an early example of a federalist system. Living in the city of Cuzo in the Andes, the supreme Sapa Inca ruled over this great array of cities and peoples. The Incas boasted a wealthy aristocracy, collective ownership of land, an efficient tax system, and sophisticated farming and food storage techniques.

The Inca cultivated a wonderful variety of crops as a result of an empire that included so many different regions, each with varying rainfall and climate. Occupying a steep terrain, the Inca mastered the art of building terraces on which to plant their crops of tomatoes, peppers, lima beans, squash, potato, maize, amaranth, several varieties of grain, and at least a dozen different types of roots and tubers. They used bird droppings, or guano, for fertilizer. They also perfected a system of raised fields—built up areas surrounded by canals that nourished the roots of the plants, drained the terraces during heavy rain, and regulated the tem-

---

WORSHIP

The Inca generally worshiped a Sun god and believed in reincarnation. Their strong moral code admonished the following: do not steal; do not lie; do not be lazy. People who adhered to this simple and uncompromising code would live in the Sun's warmth in their next life, while those who violated it would spend eternity in the cold, dark Earth.

The Inca also developed the custom of deforming the heads of infants so they would grow up to have more conical skulls. They did this by tightly wrapping a cloth around heads of newborns to change the shape of the skull. Technological accomplishments included a unique form of writing that relied on intricately knotted cords and such skill in surgery that they could cut holes in the skull to relieve pressure from head injuries. They also cultivated and relied heavily on coca leaves, chewed to reduce hunger and pain and gain extra energy at the high altitudes where they lived. Remarkable long-distance runners connected the settlements of the far-flung empire by running messages along the efficiently engineered road system.

---

perature of the fields. Some 2,000 years later, researchers have concluded that the Inca's raised fields were more efficient than modern agricultural techniques using chemical fertilizers.

Moreover, the Inca took advantage of their mountain climate to develop innovative ways of preserving food. They could freeze-dry crops simply by leaving them out for several days and covering them to protect them from dew. They then stomped on the plants to press out excess moisture and compress them. They also dried and salted meat. As a result, they kept several years' worth of food in meticulously constructed storehouses, which enabled them to both withstand the periodic *droughts* and to sustain a large army.

THE INCA CREATE MOUNTAINTOP CIVILIZATION

The Inca also achieved unprecedented mastery in stonework, taking advantage of the one resource the Andes provided in lavish abundance. The most impressive surviving example of Inca skill in construction is the remote cliff-top city of Machu Picchu, which was probably a ceremonial center and a vacation retreat for the aristocracy. Built on an 8,000-foot (2,440 m)-tall ridge overlooking a forest swathed in clouds, the city included 200 buildings that housed an estimated 1,200 people. The master Inca architects carved the stone blocks with bronze and stone tools, then smoothed them laboriously with sand. Each block was meticulously shaped to fit against the next block. Although some of the rock blocks had as many as 30 corners per block, they fit together so perfectly that even 600 years later, one cannot fit the blade of a knife between the blocks. Moreover, the Inca incorporated the rock formations of the hilltop into their design, carving sculptures and steps and constructing a beautiful and elaborate network of fountains, canals, and cisterns from the solid rock.

However, the Inca's skill in agriculture and architecture and their exquisite adaptation to their mountain homeland did them little good when they faced the invasion of the Spanish in 1526. The Spanish had already crushed the Aztec Empire to the north in Mexico. The diseases the Spanish brought to the continent—especially smallpox—debilitated the Inca, making them more vulnerable. Smallpox spread throughout the Inca Empire, killing a large percentage of the population, which had never faced the disease and so had no immunity. Perhaps fostered by the chaos of the epidemic, the Inca royal family was involved in a bitter war of succession when Francisco Pizarro arrived.

The Spanish could have been slaughtered. They had a force of 180 men with one cannon and 27 horses, while the Inca ruler Atahualpa could command 80,000 warriors. But when Atahualpa agreed to meet with the Spanish, Pizarro took him prisoner. After the Inca's supreme ruler paid a ransom that included an entire room filled with gold and twice as much silver besides, Pizarro executed him. Although Atahualpa's brother ultimately led a resistance that persisted for another 36 years, the centuries-long power of the Inca Empire was broken. The Spanish subsequently enslaved many of the Inca to work in their mines, which added to the burden of disease and despair. The population of the former empire plunged. Even now, fewer people live in the Andes than before the Spanish arrived.

GLACIERS AND CLIMATE CHANGE

Perhaps there is some irony therefore that the Andes themselves are now bearing witness to sweeping climate changes apparently brought about by the cultural and economic descendants of the silver-loving Spanish. Several recent studies of the glaciers of the Andes have provided dramatic new evidence of global warming, which most climate experts believe stems from the climate-warming impact of pollutants like carbon dioxide that trap the Sun's heat radiating off the ground.

Ohio State University *glaciologist* Lonnie Thompson has been measuring the accelerating retreat of the once-massive glaciers in the Andes for years. His measurements show that Peru's 550-foot-deep (170-m) Quelccaya ice cap is retreating 40 times faster than when it was first measured by an aerial photograph in 1963. Recently, he reported a finding that suggests the climate of the Andes is warmer now than it has been at any time in the past 50,000 years. Thompson based that conclusion on the discovery of plant remains left behind by a melting glacier. Thompson found the still frozen plants on the ground in 2002 at a spot where he had measured the front edge of a glacier the year before. He used *carbon dating* techniques on the plant samples. Such measurements are based on the observation that certain types of carbon that are absorbed by living tissues decay once the plant or animal dies. As a result, the measurement of various types of carbon in once-living tissue reveals how long ago the plant died. Thompson's measurements revealed that the plant was at least 50,000 years old. Because carbon dating techniques are unreliable in samples older than 50,000 years, it is possible that the sample was actually much older than that. He has found other plant samples abandoned by melting glaciers that were first frozen into the glacier 5,000 years ago, which means the glaciers remained stable all that time until the current planetary warming. The finding is one of the more alarming pieces of evidence suggesting a climate shift greater than any such change in the past 50,000 years. Moreover, the headlong retreat of glaciers throughout the Andes could inflict great changes on an array of ecosystems. Normally, the glaciers melt a little in the warm season and grow back in the cold season. This enables them to gradually release water vital to down-slope farmers, cities, forests, and wildlife.

Thompson's studies of the Andean glaciers—and glaciers elsewhere as well—has also contributed to growing evidence that the planet underwent a dramatic climate shift some 5,000 years ago, which might mirror current trends. Clues to that change include the preserved body of a man trapped in an Alpine glacier, ice cores from the top of the glaciers at the summit of Africa's Mount Kilimanjaro, tree ring studies from England and Ireland, the sudden shift of large areas of the Sahara into a barren desert, ice cores from Greenland and Antarctica, and pollen counts from lakes in southern Africa. No one knows for sure what might have caused that climate shift 5,000 years ago, although some experts suggest still largely unexplained variations in how much energy the Sun puts out. All of which means that the mountains that have shaped the climate of South America, sheltered the civilization of the Inca, and revealed vital clues to the history of the planet may now be harboring a deep warning in the melting trickle of its ice caps.

7

Mauna Kea, Hawaii's High Point

Pacific Ocean

Geologists thought they had Hawaii figured out. The great chain of some 20 islands large and small had been built in the course of millions of years from the quiet and predictable eruption of *volcano*es connected to a puzzling but predictable *hot spot*, presumably linked to the great currents in molten rock more than 100 miles (160 km) beneath the thin, brittle crust. The volcanoes that had built the four great

A geyser of lava from Kilauea spatters a doomed grove of palms. *(USGS)*

islands and the many small peaks steadily released fluid, slow-moving lava flows, building up the islands from the seafloor and peaking in great cone-shaped mountains like Mauna Kea, which rises 13,800 feet (4,200 m) from sea level. Mauna Kea would qualify as the world's highest mountain if measured from its base on the seafloor to its tip, a towering 33,470 feet (10,200 m). The mountain is so tall that even in this tropical zone snows gather on its summit, which was crowned with glaciers in the last ice age.

But despite all of the study of the volcanic island chain, geologists were still surprised when they first made detailed measurements of the seafloor around the islands of Oahu and Molokai. They expected to find the pronounced shelf around the islands leading to the great drop-off down to the deep ocean. But they were not prepared for the side-scan sonar measurements that revealed a massive spread of debris extending for nearly 200 miles (320 km) into the ocean around the islands. The jumble of underwater deposits evidently marked the location of a massive landslide some 100,000 years ago. Eventually, the researchers mapped the locations of 15 enormous landslides that had occurred during the past 4 million years, some so great that they must have ripped one of the island's giant volcanoes almost in half. Single underwater landslides had covered up to 2,100 square miles (5,440 km²) with a debris layer 17 to 70 feet (50–200 m) deep. Such a *cataclysm* could have triggered a 1,000-foot (300-m)-tall tidal wave that would have caused destruction half a world away.

A MOLTEN MYTHOLOGY

But if geologists were surprised by this graphic illustration of the violent and unpredictable behavior of the seemingly well-behaved volcanoes of Hawaii, maybe they just had not been studying their mythology. After all, Pele, the Hawaiian goddess most closely associated with the volcanoes of the island chain, was well known for her jealousy and unpredictable rages. The goddess of fire, lightning, dance, and volcanoes, the Pele of myth lives on the active Kilauea volcano on the Big Island near Mauna Kea. Exiled from her homeland in Tahiti because of her bad temper and her affair with her sister's husband, Pele journeyed to Hawaii guided by her brother, the god of the sharks. But her vengeful water-god elder sister pursued her, drowning each island she landed on. Pele finally turned to fight her pursuing sister near Hana on the island of Maui. Here, her older sister ripped Pele apart and scattered her bones to become geological formations. Once dead, Pele became a god and went to live on Mauna Kea, on the island of Hawaii. She had learned nothing however, and remained known for her violent temper and jealousy. Sometimes, she takes human form—either an old hag or a beautiful young woman—and goes

The snowcapped peaks and ridges of the eastern Himalayas create an irregular white-on-red patchwork between major rivers in southwestern China. The Himalayas are made up of three parallel mountain ranges that together extend more than 1,800 miles (2,900 km). *(NASA and USGS)*

Mount Mitchell in the Appalachians gathers winter storms and is the scarred survivor of millions of years of uplift and erosion. The succeeding ridges of the Appalachians shaped American history by confining the English colonists to the east coast until population densities were sufficient to support further westward expansion. *(USGS)*

The snowcapped Alps were raised by a collision between two crustal plates and now effectively form a wall across northern Italy. The presence of this geographic barrier played a key role in the development of the Roman Empire and therefore influenced the course of Western civilization. *(NASA and USGS)*

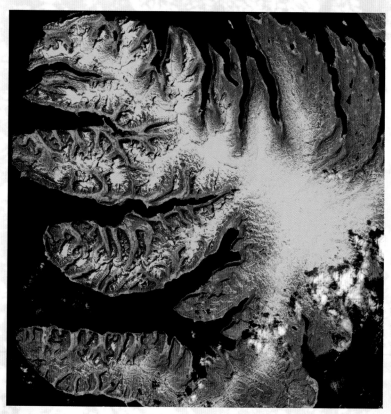

The west fjords are a series of peninsulas in northwestern Iceland, shown in the satellite image. They represent less than one-eighth of the country's land area, but their jagged perimeters account for more than half of Iceland's total coastline. *(NASA and USGS)*

In this satellite *Landstat 7* false color image, valley glaciers appear as fingers of blue ice reaching out from the Vatnajökull Glacier in Iceland's Skaftafell National Park. The park lies on the southern edge of Vatnajökull, Europe's largest ice cap. *(NASA and USGS)*

Sheet joints follow topographic surfaces to produce these nearly vertical sheets on Matthes Crest in Yosemite National Park. *(USGS)*

Yosemite's Half Dome is one of the most dramatic rock formations in the country, formed from plutons of granite that cooled far beneath the surface before the jostling of crustal plates uplifted the Sierra Nevada and erosion carried away the layers of rocks above the granite intrusions. *(USGS)*

Volcanoes that have built the Andes Mountains here mark the Chilean-Argentinean border in a false color satellite image. The Andes are the fastest rising mountain range in the world, with a near 40,000-foot (12,192-m) elevation change from the depths of the offshore Chile Trench to the highest peaks. *(NASA and USGS)*

During the April 1982 eruption of Kilauea in Hawaii Volcanoes National Park, a geologist in a protective suit makes a thermocouple of an active lava flow. *(N. Banks, USGS)*

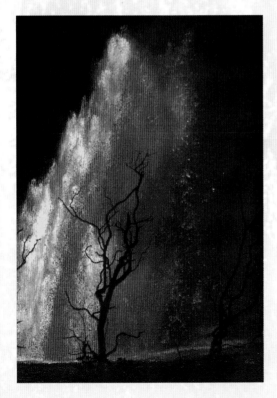

Kilauea Volcano produced this 1,000-foot (305-m) lava fountain during a major eruption in 1983. *(J. D. Griggs, USGS)*

The towering column of ash and smoke from the Mount Saint Helen's blast left a layer of fine ash that covered much of the surrounding region and drifted down to Earth hundreds of miles away. *(J. Vallance, U.S. Forest Service)*

This aerial view shows the top of the dome in the central crater of Mount Saint Helens, with a clear view of the cracks in the solid, but still hot rocks. This shot was taken in 1981, after the dome had been rebuilt. *(USGS)*

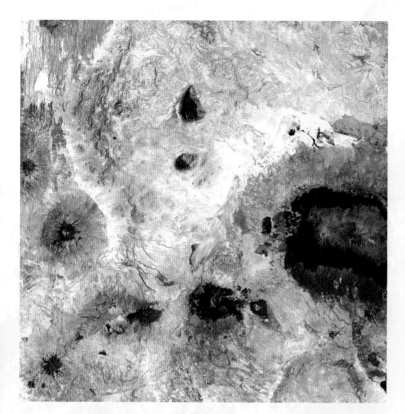

The glaciers of Kilimanjaro, the highest peak in Africa, are melting rapidly. Portions of Kenya and Tanzania can be seen in this satellite image, with the peak of Kilimanjaro on the right. The plains of Amboseli National Park to the north and the rugged Arusha National Park to the south and west flank the mountain. *(NASA and USGS)*

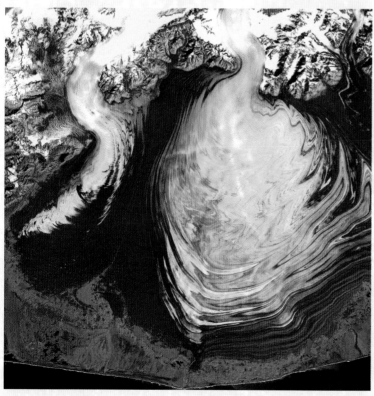

Glaciers have been melting rapidly in many areas all over the world, including Alaska. Here, most of the image shows the tongue of the Malaspina Glacier, which with an area of 1,500 square miles (3,880 km^2) is the largest in Alaska. *(NASA and USGS)*

Humphreys Peak is the highest mountain of the San Francisco Peaks, the remains of a volcano that blew off the top third of the mountain in a cataclysmic explosion. The highest point in Arizona, the mountain rises from the surrounding desert, creating such a dramatic change in habitat with elevation that original theories of different life zones were developed here. *(Peter Aleshire)*

Some 800 years ago, adaptable farming people known as the Sinagua used sandstone blocks to construct this settlement, now preserved as part of Wupatki National Monument in Arizona. The ashfall from the seemingly catastrophic explosion of nearby Sunset Crater actually improved the growing conditions and led to a population boom. *(Peter Aleshire)*

among the people of the islands. Often, she travels with a white dog. She tests people by asking for food or a ride to the other side of the island. Kind people reap rewards, but mean, selfish people often find their homes destroyed and crops aflame. When enraged, she appears as pure flame. The vocabulary of volcanology includes many references to this fiery goddess. Droplets of lava are Pele's Tears. Those droplets are often found attached to Pele's Hair, fine golden strands of volcanic glass.

This fascinating web of myth, geology, history, and ecology makes Hawaii one of the most unusual showcases for the forces that have shaped the planet. The existence of this towering mountain chain in the middle of the Pacific Ocean has provided the perfect place for geologists to study the behavior of volcanoes and has contributed significantly to the understanding of plate tectonics and the makeup of the workings of the planet. The recent discovery of the underwater landslides has added an ominous new chapter to this long study of the capricious and violent potential for cataclysm that lies behind Pele's beautiful face.

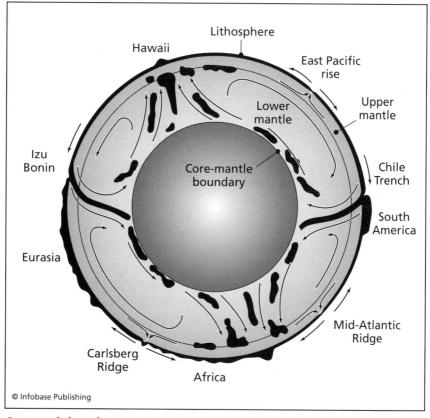

Core-mantle boundary

THE BEST-STUDIED HOT SPOT

The Hawaiian Islands remain the best-studied example of a hot spot, a fixed area of volcanic activity that can persist for millions of years. (See color insert on page C-5.) Some 18 islands comprise the Hawaiian Islands, most of them uninhabited outcrops of volcanic rock that barely break the surface. The bulk of the above-ocean land area is concentrated on four islands—Kaui, Oahu, Maui, and Hawaii. By far the largest and youngest island, Hawaii has been built up by the eruptions of five current volcanoes. (See color insert on page C-5.) Kilauea, Mauna Loa, and Hualalai have each erupted in the past 200 years, while Mauna Kea is considered *dormant*. The only other above-water volcano in the chain to erupt in the past 300 years is Haleakala on the island of Maui.

The Hawaiian Islands lie at the southernmost end of a chain of volcanoes now covered by the Pacific Ocean in a 3,700-mile-long (6,000-km) arch stretching from the Big Island of Hawaii to the Aleutian Trench off Alaska. This mountain chain was caused by a single geologic hot spot that has been heating the underside of the Pacific crustal plate for the past 70 million years. The Pacific Plate moves steadily over this hot spot at about the rate human fingernails grow as *magma* pushes to the surface along an undersea ridge system on one side and descends into a system of undersea trenches on the other. This Hawaiian Ridge–Emperor Seamounts chain includes 80 major volcanoes, most of them deep beneath the ocean's surface and long extinct. The Hawaiian Ridge segment alone stretches from Hawaii to Midway Island, nearly the width of the continental United States. The 179,935 cubic miles (750,000 km³) of rock that have erupted in this chain of volcanoes could cover the state of California with a layer of rock one mile deep.

The idea of a hot spot was first coined in 1963 by J. Tuzon Wilson, a geologist who played a key role in the development of the theory of plate tectonics, which has revolutionized geology in the past half century. Geologists believe hot spots are driven by the complex makeup of the currents in the molten and semimolten rocks of the *mantle*. Early theories suggested perhaps a single heated *plume* made its way all the way up from the molten core, through the mantle, and to the surface. More recent hypotheses have focused on convection currents in the upper reaches of the mantle. Some geologists now speculate that hot spots might actually be the result of a hole punched in the thin crust by the impact of the sort of giant asteroid thought to be responsible for different mass extinctions in the Earth's history. This theory holds that a big enough asteroid might create a weak spot in the crust, which would then trigger the creation of a hot spot. Afterwards, the hot spot would be self-sustaining, driven by the molten, intensely pressurized rock moving up through the flaw in the crust to the surface at the point of impact. Whatever the cause, geologists

YELLOWSTONE HOT SPOT: A TITANIC EXPLOSION

Although hot spots generally produce quiet and well-behaved volcanoes like those that have built Hawaii atop the ocean floor, the hot spot thought to have created the geological wonders of Yellowstone may have produced the most titanic volcanic explosion in history. Lava from the Yellowstone hot spot first reached the surface some 17 million years ago as successive eruptions covered much of Washington, Oregon, Nevada, Idaho, and even California with lava. Geologists are still debating the origins of the hot spot. Most suspect a connection to the molten rocks of the Earth's mantle. Some say that an asteroid impact might have triggered the formation of the hot spot, which then buried all evidence of the crater. Interestingly, the formation of the Yellowstone hot spot coincides with the onset of massive volcanic activity in the Pacific Northwest. In any case, the Yellowstone hot spot created a chain of *calderas* stretching halfway across North America, comparable to today's Hawaiian Ridge-Emperor Seamount chain. The movement of the hot spot as the continent drifted overhead created much of the modern landscape of the West.

Geologists have found evidence for at least three titanic Yellowstone explosions in the past 2 million years. Individually, these eruptions were about 2,500 times more powerful than the eruption of Mount Saint Helens in 1980. The most recent, some 640,000 years ago, produced a layer of ash that covered most of North America. These massive explosions along with the much smaller periods of increased activity that come once every 20,000 years are all driven by magma gathered in a huge chamber far beneath the surface. This molten rock is permeated by dissolved elements that would instantly explode into gas form except for the pressure of the overlying rock. If a geological shift reduces that pressure even slightly, it causes a chain-reaction explosion as the dissolved elements in the molten rock convert to gas. Those three eruptions were each considered "mega-colossal" on the Volcanic Explosivity Index. A repeat today could kill millions and affect the climate of the entire planet. Other such mega-colossal eruptions have been associated with mass extinctions planetwide.

have identified some 50 hot spots worldwide, most prominently Hawaii, Iceland in the Atlantic Ocean, Yellowstone in North America, Réunion Island in the Indian Ocean, and the Galápagos Island in the Pacific Ocean.

The five major volcanoes that built Hawaii comprise the southeastern cluster of a chain that began to form 70 million years ago when the hot spot formed. Most of these volcanoes long ago sank beneath the ocean as the movement of the crustal plates over the fixed location of the hot spot deprived them of the lava needed to keep building them up. The five major Hawaiian volcanoes to have erupted in the past 200 years include Kilauea, Mauna Loa, and Hualalai. The youngest volcano in the chain, Loihi, remains 3,000 feet (910 m) beneath the surface. One other Hawaiian volcano—Haleakala on the island of Maui—has erupted since the 1600s.

The volcanic chain that includes at least 80 extinct, undersea volcanoes stretches for some 6,000 miles (9,660 km) from Hawaii to the Aleutian Trench off the coast of Alaska, where one edge of the Pacific Plate descends beneath the neighboring crustal plate. Geologists estimate

A road sign offers an ironically appropriate warning as a slow-motion, 1969 lava flow moves down the flanks of Kilauea Volcano. *(USGS)*

that building the active section of the Hawaiian Ridge required enough lava to bury the entire state of California beneath a layer of rock one mile deep.

A VOLCANIC LANDSCAPE

On the Hawaiian Islands this slow, steady outpouring of lava has created one of the most vivid and contorted volcanic landscapes on Earth. Although the Hawaiian volcanoes have sometimes unleashed massive eruptions, as evidenced by the staggering size of the undersea landslides that radiate outward from the islands, these volcanoes fed by a steady, thick source of lava usually behave themselves. In fact, Hawaii remains perhaps the safest place on Earth to grab a ringside seat to a volcanic outpouring. Although the slow, superheated flow of molten rock sometimes consumes homes and tropical forests, the lava rarely moves fast enough to overtake fleeing humans or animals. Volcanologists have adopted many native Hawaiian words to describe characteristics of volcanoes. For instance, *pahoehoe* is a smooth or ropey textured lava flow and `a`a (pronounced ah-ah) is a rough, broken-surfaced flow. Reportedly, `a`a comes from the sound a barefoot person would make crossing such a flow. *Pahoehoe* means "smooth and unbroken."

Study of the Hawaiian volcanoes has revealed much about the inner workings of volcanoes and their contribution to mountain-building.

The chemistry and behavior of the volcanoes changes as they age from the young, preshield phase (like Loihi), through the development as full-fledged *shield volcanoes* (like Kilauea) and finally to the dying, postshield volcanoes like Haleakala. Moreover, once-quiet volcanoes sometimes awaken with an outpouring of lava of distinct behavior and chemistry, like Diamond Head on Oahu. The enormous weight of the huge cones of lava six miles (10 km) tall rising from the seafloor actually causes the crust on which they sit to sag and slump, which means that peaks built tall enough to become islands sink once again beneath the waves after fresh lava stops building up their summits. Without the lava to add to their height, the weight of the islands bows the crust beneath so that they return to the ocean from which they rose. Often, extensive coral reefs will grow on top of these drowned mountains, although rapid changes in sea level due to global climate changes can kill even these gigantic reef systems. Currently, reef systems around Hawaii on sunken seamounts have been designated a national wildlife refuge and shelter some of the most colorful and various ocean life on the planet. Many of those reefs could be threatened by a too-rapid rise in sea level predicted by some models of global warming.

The Hawaiian Islands now harbor a variety of dramatic volcanic landscapes, like Diamond Head. Perhaps the most famous formation on any of the islands, Diamond Head formed on Oahu some 100,000 years ago as a result of a series of volcanic explosions. The island itself began forming about 3 million years ago and grew from the merger of two great shield volcanoes. The volcanic activity that built up the island came in phases, the most recent roughly one million years ago with an explosion of heated ash that fell to the ground to form the welded tufts—fused volcanic ash. Some 300,000 years ago such an explosion of ash out of a broad, 350-acre (140-ha) crater that pointed seaward created Diamond Head. A coral reef formed on the ocean side of the blasted open crater, which is considered a vivid example of a volcanic tuft cone.

The islands also boast the world's largest active volcano, the massive Mauna Loa. With a volume of more than 9,500 cubic miles (40,000 km^3), the sheer mass of lava makes the seafloor beneath the surface sag. The bulk of the volcano is composed entirely of thin flows of aa and pahoehoe, each layer perhaps 12 feet (4 m) thick. Repeatedly, lava breaks out of vents scattered on the flanks and summit of the massive volcano, forming rivers of lava that are perhaps 0.6 miles (1 km) wide and often 30 miles (50 km) long. The mountain is topped by a caldera about 2.5 miles (4 km) wide and 590 feet (180 m) deep. Although the often snow-capped mountain rises a modest 15,400 feet (4,690 m) above sea level, that above-water peak sits on top of a 5.6 mile (9 km) tall submerged base.

Another important Hawaiian volcano remains well beneath the ocean's surface, perhaps the beginning of another island in the chain. Loihi, the youngest major volcano in the Hawaiian chain, has already forced changes in geologists' understanding of the nature of the great seamounts scattered across the ocean floor. The existence of such underwater mountains, often with tops seemingly flattened by wave action, baffled geologists before the development of the theory of plate tectonics explained their enigmatic presence.

Taller than Mount Saint Helens in the Cascade Range back on the mainland, geologists assumed that Loihi was an extinct volcano that had sunk beneath the surface. However, in 1970 the seamount surprised almost everyone by unleashing a swarm of small earthquakes. An expedition to study the seamount discovered that it was actually a young, active volcano, with many hydrothermal vents on and around the summit. These vents spewed out superheated, mineral-rich water along deep fractures in the seamount's structure. Many of those vents release water heated to 390°F (200°C). In 1996, Loihi underwent a series of eruptions and has remained fitfully active ever since. The movement of the magma continues to cause earthquakes and eruptions, with most of the earthquakes centered between 7.5 to 173 miles (12 and 28 km) beneath the surface. That is well above the boundary between the light, brittle rock of the crust and the dense, semimolten rock of the Earth's mantle.

MAUNA KEA: THE TALLEST MOUNTAIN

Mauna Kea is the tallest mountain in the chain, which makes it the tallest mountain on the planet when measured from its base on the seafloor. Located on the island of Hawaii, it rises to 13,800 feet (4,200 m) above sea level on top of its 5.6-mile (9-km) base. That gives the volcano a total height of 33,470 feet (10,200 m). Now considered dormant, Mauna Kea has not erupted in about 4,000 years. The mountain still carries the scars of the ice age glaciers that adorned its peaks off and on for 200,000 years, as still poorly understood climate shifts caused a succession of ice ages that ended some 11,000 years ago. Near the summit is a distinctive deposit of dense rock that geologists believe formed when molten rock emerging from a volcanic vent was quenched by direct contact with the thick ice of a glacier. The snows of its summit prompted its name, which means "White Mountain" in Hawaiian. Once popular with snowboarders and skiers near its summit, locals now blame frequent snowless winters on global warming.

Far from city lights, the still, cool air at the top of Mauna Kea is perfect for telescopes, since it minimizes the distortions caused by the dance of the *atmosphere* at lower elevations. As a result, astronomers have built one of the world's most powerful telescopes on its summit. Because the summit stands above 40 percent of the Earth's atmosphere and 90 percent of its heavy water vapor, the telescope produces exceptionally clear images. Taking advantage of 300 nights of clear skies each year, astronomers atop Mauna Kea at 20°N latitude can glimpse much of both the northern and southern skies. Perched on a dead volcano forged by the fires of the planet beneath their feet, astronomers have made breakthrough discoveries about stars and other distant planets.

However, the crowding of observatories on top of the mountain has angered many native Hawaiians, who consider the peak sacred. Native Hawaiian groups have repeatedly protested the construction of new telescopes, which inevitably involve grading of the *cinder cone* landscape. Native Hawaiians say Mauna Kea is home of Poliahu, the snow goddess. Sacred to the Hawaiians with their rich stories of Pele and her implacable relatives, the mountain also harbors an array of unique but endangered plants and animals, including the Wekiu bug, the Palila bird and the Mauna Kea Silversword, a spiky plant. The tiny Wekiu bug lives in the snow where it dines on insects blown up from the warm base of the mountain and immobilized by the cold at the top. The windward, eastern slopes are covered with a dense rain forest that overlooks farmland once planted with sugar cane. After the sugar cane industry collapsed in the 1990s due to international competition and the rise of artificial sweeteners, growers planted the well-watered area around the foot of the mountain with eucalyptus trees for wood pulp and grass for cattle. Like most areas of Hawaii, the mountain and its native plants and animals have suffered from an invasion of foreign species, which gives Hawaii more endangered native species per square mile than any place in the world.

THE FIRST HAWAIIANS

People first reached Hawaii in about 1000 C.E., brave settlers from the Polynesian Islands far across the Pacific. Just finding the speck of volcanic rock in the midst of the great ocean was a remarkable accomplishment. Only the Easter Islands are further from any other mainland than Hawaii. These settlers lived in isolation on the remote, lush island for some 800 years, establishing a complex caste society dominated by warring chiefdoms and elaborate religious and social taboos.

Europeans first came across Hawaii in the 1700s, which they initially dubbed the Sandwich Islands. British explorer James Cook stumbled upon the islands in 1778, although historians now believe that Spanish ships probably reached the islands before him. The British helped one chief gradually gain control over the all the major islands for the first time in Hawaiian history. The kingdom that Kamehameha established in 1810 lasted until 1893, when a coup led by American and European planters overthrew the last Hawaiian monarch. The coup opened the way for the domination of the island by American growers, who produced some 200,000 tons of sugar annually. Hawaii was annexed by the United States in 1898 and became a state in 1959.

Several legends revolve around Poliahu, the goddess of snow and water associated with the peak. In one, she fell in love with another sacred being only to discover that he was already engaged to the princess of Maui. Outraged, Poliahu cursed her rival—first chilling her, then turning the cold to heat. Then she cursed her would-be lover, freezing him to death. His foolish rejection of her is hard to understand, since she was considered the most beautiful goddess of Hawaii. Another myth recounts how Poliahu mingled with the human beings who lived on the eastern slope of Mauna Kea, an area of such lush beauty and many streams that Hawaiians say she made it herself. But one day while Poliahu was sledding with mortals, a beautiful stranger challenged her. Having no sled, the mysterious beauty borrowed one to race against the goddess. Poliahu easily beat the stranger on the first race, but when someone commented that she simply had the better sled she changed sleds. Once again, the snow goddess won the race. On the third round, the stranger urged Poliahu to go first—then suddenly caused lava streams to open up in front of her. Suddenly, everyone realized that the beautiful stranger was Pele, the goddess of fire. Poliahu fled toward the top of the mountain, seeking the elements that gave her power. There, she regained her courage and turned to hurl snow at the pursuing lava and froze it, which solidified the distinctive landscape of the island's southern end. So now, while Pele rules the still fuming and active Kilauea and Mauna Loa, Poliahu holds sway on the snowcapped Mauna Kea and the northern end of the island.

8

Mount Saint Helens

Northwestern United States

May 18, 1980, dawned clear and bright, another perfect day on Spirit Lake—a pristine, beautiful lake in the shadow of the volcanic Mount Saint Helens. Harry Truman savored the day, as he had done almost every day for the past 54 years. Most of his life, he had lived at the foot of the fitful *volcano* so perfectly formed that it was considered the Fuji of North America. But after a long slumber, the mountain had awakened and now it jittered with small earthquakes as it steamed and hissed sulfur fumes. In the middle of its huge central crater had grown a dome of lava higher than the Empire State Building.

Geologists and state disaster planning officials had sought a voluntary evacuation from all around the mountain. The volcanologists who had flocked to this most active of the *Cascades Range* volcanoes for a front-row seat to geological history could not predict whether the mountain would erupt or merely sputter and fume. But Harry had ignored the orders to evacuate, saying he did not want to live anywhere but Spirit Lake, a high-altitude basin abounding in fish and wildlife with the snow-capped Saint Helens reflected in its deep, cold waters. So Harry stayed, watching the mountain and granting seemingly endless interviews to the newspaper and television reporters who had flocked to the area for the big show.

Up on a ridge a safe distance from the smoking mountain sat volcanologist David A. Johnston, who was making meticulous observations of the site through his telescope. The 30-year-old volcano expert was having the time of his life, watching a great volcano come to life. Saint Helens promised to be one of the most carefully monitored volcanoes in history, since the Cascades Range was the most active and dangerous volcanic area in North America.

CASCADES: EDGE OF A CRUSTAL PLATE

The Cascades extend for 1,000 miles (1,610 km), from southern British Columbia to northern California. Seven of the 160 active volcanoes in

Aerial view of Mount Saint Helens looking northeast hours after the start of the eruption. The day had dawned clear, and clouds in this scene may be eruption related. Vapor rises from vents and from lakes, rivers, melted snow and ice, and from hot deposits of debris avalanche and pyroclastic flows. Ash billows from a vent and from pulverized material collapsing into a crater. Smoke originates from forest fires ignited by initial eruptive blasts and from later pyroclastic flows. Lightning was occurring every few seconds. No air turbulence was felt on windward side of the mountain. *(R. M. Krimmel, USGS)*

this long chain have erupted in the past 200 years, four of them recently enough to have caused considerable property damage. The chain is the direct result of the offshore collision between three crustal plates, with one plate driven down beneath the other two. The buried crustal plate melts as it is forced down into the hot, pressurized earth. The expansion of the less dense melted rock exerts fierce pressure on the overlying crust and finds its way back to the surface through faults and fissures. This escaping, supercharged *magma* has built this great chain of mountains in the past 40 million years, making it one of the most volcanically active zones in the world. Unfortunately, Harry underestimated this volcano. And perhaps more surprisingly, so did Johnston.

The mountain had been rumbling and fuming for months, as magma made its way up from great depths to collect in a great *magma chamber* beneath the summit. The mountain had erupted repeatedly in historical times, but it had been quiet long enough that people were more curious than fearful when it rumbled back to life. The magma was made from the melted rocks of the *subduct*ed crustal plate, which means it had a high concentration of both water and carbon dioxide. The accumulated magma caused a bulge in the volcano's north side, pushing upwards and outwards over 450 feet (140 m).

The mountain announced its latest active phase with a 5.1 magnitude earthquake on March 20, 1980, a rumbling of the earth caused by the movement of magma up from great depths. By the end of April, the north side of the mountain had begun to bulge from the internal pressure of the magma, steam, and gas. On May 18, a second 5.1 magnitude earthquake caused a landslide on the strained north side of the mountain. The avalanche of rock and dirt thinned the side of the mountain just enough to unleash a *cataclysm.* The whole north face collapsed into the expanding magma chamber. In an instant, the pressure that had contained that superheated slurry of gas and molten rock was released. Standing on Coldwater Ridge directly opposite the north face, Johnston watched the collapse and the massive eruption. "Vancouver! Vancouver! This is it," he cried into his radio a moment before the blast of gas and ash and molten rock reached his ridge. His body was never found. He had witnessed close up the beginning of the sort of event he had spent his whole life imagining—the largest recorded debris avalanche in recorded history. Turned to something between a solid and a gas by the pressurized steam and carbon dioxide, the collapse of the north face unleashed a massive *pyroclastic* flow that was pointed at the surrounding forest and ridgeline, rather than directed up into the sky. The blast flattened vegetation and buildings over a 230-square-mile area (600-km^2). But even worse was to come. The explosion almost immediately melted the great mass of snow and ice that covered the summit of the then 9,680-foot (2,950-m) mountain. The mix of magma, ash, water, and ice created a massive lahar, a volcanic mudflow. These devastating lahars rushed for miles down the Toutle and Cowlitz Rivers, obliterating buildings and timber camps. Some 105.9 million cubic feet (3 million m^3) was transported 17 miles (27 km) to clog the great Columbia River with mudflows. In moments, the explosion and the avalanche of mud and ash had killed 57 people, including Harry Truman. The wall of mud crashed into Spirit Lake, completely devastating it. All told, the eruption destroyed 250 homes, 47 bridges, 15 miles (24 km) of railways, and 185 miles (300 km) of highways in the course of inflicting

EFFECTS OF MOUNT SAINT HELENS ERUPTION

+ Blew off the top 1,314 feet (400 m) of the mountain
+ Ejected 0.67 cubic miles (2.8 km³) of rock and ash
+ Created a 1.8-mile (2.90-km)-wide crater
+ Produced a 23-square-mile (60 km²) landslide
+ Buried a 14-mile (23 km) long river valley to an average depth of 150 feet (46 m)
+ Spawned 150-mile (240 km)-per-hour landslides
+ Lateral blast affected 230 square miles (600 km²), up to 17 miles (27 km) from the crater
+ The speed of rock and ash blasted from the crater reached 300 miles (480 km) an hour.
+ The ejected rock reached temperatures as high as 660°F (350°C).
+ The blast released 24 megatons of thermal energy.
+ The blast knocked down 4 billion board feet of timber, enough to build 300,000 homes.
+ The lahar mudslides reached speeds of up to 50 miles (80 km) an hour and damaged 27 bridges and 200 homes.
+ The mud reduced the depth of the distant Columbia River from 40 to 14 feet (12 to 4 m), stranding more than 24 ships.
+ The explosive column of ash reached a height of 80,000 feet (24,400 m) in just three minutes.
+ The .26 cubic miles of ash covered a 22,000-square-mile (57,000 km²) area and reached a depth of about 10 inches (25 cm) 10 miles (16 km) downwind and a depth of one inch at a distance of 300 miles (480 km).
+ The pyroclastic flows reached speeds of 80 miles (130 km) an hour and covered 6 square miles (15.5 km²).
+ The depth of the 1,300°F (700°C) pyroclastic flow deposits reached 120 feet (40 m) in some places.
+ The eruption killed 57 people, 7,000 big game animals, and at least 12 million salmon in hatcheries.

Source: U.S. Geological Survey

The first moments of the fatal eruption of Mount Saint Helens in 1980 in what will become a towering column of ash out of the side of the volcano (USGS)

Aerial view of edge of blast zone on Mount Saint Helens, which left an almost definite line between standing and downed trees. Even the standing trees were killed by the blast. *(USGS)*

an estimated $1 billion in damages. It also killed an estimated 7,000 deer, bear, and elk, and at least 12 million fish in a hatchery were consumed by the lahars.

The immediate explosion was followed by a towering plume of black, roiling volcanic ash, which rose like a mushroom cloud for thousands of feet. The plume of ash billowed for more than nine hours after the eruption, reaching a height of 16 miles (27 km) and moving eastward at a speed of about 60 miles (100 km) an hour. (See upper color insert on page C-6.) By noon, ash had begun to settle in distant Idaho. Seattle and Portland would be cleaning up the thick, sticky, abrasive ash for weeks to come. The eruption and the ash cloud together released 0.67 cubic miles (2.8 km³) of material. In the wake of the explosion, President Jimmy Carter commented that, "someone said this area looked like a moonscape. But the Moon looks more like a golf course compared to what's up there."

Incredibly enough, even after the explosion a film crew decided to get as close as possible. A helicopter dropped Seattle filmmaker Otto Seiber and his camera crew on the mountain to document the devastation. But as soon as they touched down, they noticed that their compasses were swinging wildly about in circles—unhinged by the magnetic properties of the rock around and beneath them. A second eruption took place while they were on the mountain, but fortunately they survived to be rescued two days later by National Guard helicopters.

All told, Saint Helens had released energy equivalent to 350 mega-tons of dynamite—or about 27,000 times as much energy as the atom bomb that destroyed Hiroshima. The eruption blasted off the top 1,300 feet (400 m) of the mountain. The 0.7 cubic mile (2.9 km³) debris flow qualifies as the largest in recorded history, although there is geological evidence of much larger debris flows that were never recorded in historical accounts. The eruption reduced the summit to about 8,000 feet (2,440 m), leaving in its place a horseshoe-shaped, mile-wide crater. In fact, Saint Helens also qualifies as the most economically damaging volcanic eruption in the history of the United States, although ancient cataclysms created much larger volcanic outbursts and even in recent times the eruption of remote Mount Katmai in Alaska qualified as a larger eruption. Despite the fury of its outburst, Mount Saint Helens actually qualifies as only a middling peak among more than 100 volcanoes in the Cascade Range. Eruptions began building the mountain a mere 40,000 years ago, a blink of an eye in geologic time. Saint Helens' perfectly formed pre-eruption peak rose some 5,000 feet (1,520 m) above its base just 2,200 years ago.

A VIOLENT HISTORY

Even though the actual 1980 explosion proved lethally unpredictable, both geologists and Native American groups that have lived in the area for thousands of years understood the potential fury of the volcano. People have lived near the volcano for at least 6,500 years and have often had to adjust to the mountain's outbursts. Some 3,500 years ago, an eruption buried many Indian settlements under a thick layer of ash, which probably forced the abandonment of the area for the next 2,000 years, according to *archeological* studies.

More recent groups have told intricate stories to account for the volcanic outbursts. The Klickitats tell the story of the Bridge of the Gods, which involves the chief of the gods and his two sons, who traveled down the Columbia River seeking a place to settle. When his sons began to quarrel, their father sent them to live in different places in the mountains. But then the two boys fell in love with a beautiful maiden named Loowit, who refused to make a choice between them. So the two gods fought for her, burying many villages and forests in their struggle. They fought so violently that they destroyed a great bridge their father had built to let them visit one another, which shattered and fell in pieces to create the cascades of the Columbia River Gorge. Furious at the destruction, their father transformed each of the lovers into mountains. One son became Mount Hood, another became Mount Adams, and the beautiful girl became Saint Helens, whose native name among the Klickitats means "fire mountain."

AN EXPLOSIVE HISTORY OF MOUNT SAINT HELENS

+ 40,000–35,000 years ago: Mount Saint Helens begins to form, building up a towering, cone-shaped mountain.
+ 20,000–18,000 years ago: Active explosions in the Cougar stage
+ 13,000–8,000 years ago: Explosions common in the Swift Creek stage. In these three early stages, lava consisted mostly of dacite and andesite.
+ 4,500 years ago: Modern period of eruptions noted as the Spirit Lake stage started after a 4,000-year-long dormant period.
+ 1900 B.C.E.: The largest known eruption ejected some 2.5 cubic miles (10 km³) of rock and ash, followed by a dormant period lasting 400 years.
+ 1200 B.C.E.: The Pine Creek period lasted for 400 years and was marked by smaller eruptions, although one mudflow filled a 40-mile (64-km)-long river valley.
+ 400 B.C.E.: The Castle Creek period was marked by a change in the composition of the lava, with the addition of olivine basalt.
+ 100 C.E.: The brief Sugar Bowl eruptive period produced the only other known lateral blast from the mountain, which means the explosion closely resembled the 1980 blast.
+ 1480–1800 C.E.: The Kalama and Goat Rocks eruptions shattered a 700-year period of dormancy with an outburst several times as large as the 1980 event. Some 10 miles (16 km) from the volcano, the ash piled up in a three-foot (.90-m)-thick layer. An explosion in 1800 rivaled the size of the 1980 eruption.

Explorers heard distant reports of a volcanic mountain in the 1800s, which coincided with a 57-year-long active period. The members of Lewis and Clark Expedition in 1805 reported sighting the distant peak. Although they did not witness an explosion, they did make note of the evidence of recent eruptions in the main channel of the Columbia River. The first eyewitness account of an eruption was made by Dr. Meredith Gairdner in 1835, while he was working for the fur-trading Hudson Bay Company. The next recorded eruption was in 1842, when settlers and missionaries recorded the "Great Explosion," which produced small outbursts of ash clouds and blasts for about 15 years. One outburst in 1842 created an ash cloud that settled some 50 miles away (80 km). Another eruption with an attendant ash cloud was reported in 1857.

The mountain has remained fitfully active ever since the 1980 explosion. A new lava *dome* immediately begin forming in the center of the central crater as magma from great depths continued to push towards the surface. Often, the growth of the dome in the crater was attended by an outpouring of smoke and ash. (See lower color insert on page C-6.)

On October 1, 2004, Mount Saint Helens entered a new, more active phase, with thousands of localized earthquakes and significant columns of steam and ash. Some five months later, a bizarre formation dubbed the "whaleback" whose height would eventually dwarf the Empire State Building began rising from the floor of the giant crater left by the 1980 explosion. This lava dome was comprised of long shafts of cooling magma, squeezed-up from beneath the floor of the crater. These strange, squeezed up formations often shattered under their own weight. Eventually the tip of the whaleback broke off, causing a rockfall and a huge cloud of dust. The whaleback even grew a "fin," a chunk of rock the size of a football field that was pushed upwards as much as 6 feet (2 m) per day, before it finally crumbled. Then in March 2005, the mountain unleashed a 36,000-foot (11,000-m)-tall column of ash visible in distant Seattle, accompanied by a 2.5 magnitude earthquake.

CASCADES SUPPORT PLATE TECTONICS

All this furious activity originates deep beneath the surface and the effort to unravel the puzzle of the smoking, belching, exploding volcanoes of the Cascades played a key role in shaping modern theories of plate tectonics, which now explain many geological mysteries. Saint Helens and the other violent volcanoes of the Cascades Range all draw their fire from the collision of crustal plates and the aftereffects of the destruction of a huge chunk of the Earth's crust, forced down beneath larger crustal plates. Just off the coast, the North American Plate bumps up against the San Juan De Fuca Plate along a jagged fracture on the seafloor. Coincidentally, the study of that fractured crust on the seafloor played a key role in the development of the theory of plate tectonics, which is perhaps the single most influential theory in the history of geology.

It started when a research ship from the Scripps Institute of Oceanography steamed over the fracture zone towing along behind a magnetometer, designed to make measurements of the magnetic features on the seafloor. Geologists had noticed odd strips of reversed magnetic polarity on both sides of the massive undersea mountain range known as the Mid-Atlantic Ridge. Geologists had no good explanation for the perplexing magnetic stripes, but they began routinely surveying the seafloor searching for other such anomalies.

The magnetometer towed behind the Scripps vessel made some very strange readings—a zebra-stripe pattern hidden beneath thick layers of mud emptied into the ocean by the Columbia River. Those measurements ultimately led to the evolution of the theory of plate tectonics, which neatly explains the long chain of volcanoes in the Cascades. Geophysicists realized that the matching magnetic strips that occur on both sides of major *fissures* and ridges, like the San Juan De Fuca fracture zone, formed when molten magma reaches the surface along a great crack in

VOLCANIC MOUNTAINS OF THE CASCADES

✦ Mount Adams, Washington: One of the largest mountains in the chain, it has great potential for destruction but has not erupted in several thousand years.

✦ Mount Baker, Washington: This 10,780-foot-tall (3,290 m) volcano is covered in 0.43 cubic miles (1.8 km3) of ice, more than all the other Cascades peaks combined—not counting Mount Rainier.

✦ Crater Lake, Oregon: The collapse of a 12,000-foot (3,700 m) mountain some 7,700 years ago left a deep crater that filled with water thanks to winter snows averaging 550 inches (1,400 cm) per year. Crater Lake is 1,960 feet (600 m) deep, making it the deepest in the United States and the seventh deepest in the world. Trapped in the five-mile (8-km)-diameter crater with walls that tower 2,000 feet (610 m) above it's surface, the lake also boasts a small central cinder cone (a pile of rock from a vent) that rises some 760 feet (230 m) above it.

✦ Mount Garibaldi, British Columbia: Violent eruptions built this mountain between 15,000 and 20,000 years ago, but it has fallen silent in the past 10,000 years.

✦ Glacier Peak, Washington: One of the five most active Cascades volcanoes, the mountain's remote location makes it less of a threat to human lives and property than Saint Helens. Since the last ice age, the volcano has produced six major explosions, including one just 300 years ago.

✦ Mount Hood, Oregon: Close by Portland, Mount Hood has erupted repeatedly in the past few thousand years. Although the most recent eruption dates back to the time of the Lewis and Clark Expedition, the volcano's proximity to a major city makes it one of the most potentially dangerous of the Cascade volcanoes.

✦ Lassen Peak, California: Along with Saint Helens, Lassen is the most recently active of the Cascades volcanoes. The landscape includes great lava pinnacles, craters, vents, glacier-cut valleys, sparkling lakes, and gushing streams.

✦ Medicine Lake, California: The largest volcano in the whole range, the mountain was built by thick, gentle, persistent lava flows. Some 150 miles (240 km) across and 7,900 feet (2,410 m) high, this volcano is unique in the range because several small magma chambers feed into the central crater.

✦ Mount Rainier, Washington: The glacier-covered mountain has been erupting off and on for 500,000 years, making it more than 10 times as old as Saint Helens. Towering to 14,140 feet (4,310 m), the mountain's coastal location means it gets a lot of rain, which feeds its many glaciers. The mountain has erupted as recently as the 1840s and a fresh eruption could trigger massive lahars and floods.

✦ Mount Shasta, California: One of the largest peaks in the Cascades Range, Mount Shasta is a dormant massive stratovolcano built in the past 100,000 years by overlapping cones from at least four main vents.

the crust. When the magma cools, magnetic elements in the rock are locked into position oriented towards the North Pole.

Fortunately for geologists trying to piece together plate tectonics, the Earth's pole periodically flips, so that north becomes south. This accounts for the stripes of alternating magnetic polarity. Each reversal of the poles is reflected in the magnetic orientation of the magma as it reaches the surface and hardens between two crustal plates. Moreover, geologists have dated the pole-flips going back for millions of years. That means the magnetic stripes along crustal plate edges can help date the movement of the crustal plates themselves. This revelation proved crucial in reconstructing past movements of the plates and the continents. In fact, the Earth's poles may be in the process of flipping right now, since the Earth's magnetic field appears to have weakened by 10 or 15 percent in the past 150 years. The precise cause of such a pole flipping remains unclear, but it probably has something to do with the convection currents in Earth's core. A magnetic pole reversal probably takes about 2,000 years to complete. The poles last flipped 780,000 years ago, a bit longer than the 500,000-year average—although sometimes the poles do not flip for up to 35 million years.

Several geologists had already developed the framework for a theory to explain how the division of the planet's surface into crustal plates could account for the movement of the continents and for volcanoes like Saint Helens. Canadian geologist J. Tuzo Wilson set out to explain why islands in the Pacific, including Hawaii, got older the further removed they were from the East Pacific Rise. Wilson suggested that the East Pacific Rise formed the edge of a crustal plate and offered a detailed model for how the process actually worked. Wilson realized that instead of creating a single crack, the plate edge would break up into hundreds of shorter sections, each offset by smaller fault lines. So while the crust would pull apart along the crack itself, two pieces of crust could also slip past one another along one of these offsetting faults. He cited the *San Andreas Fault* in California, as an example. This massive, deadly crack in the Earth runs from the narrow Gulf of California all the way up the coast of California and then plunges into the ocean. As it turns out, it lines up quite nicely with the San Juan de Fuca Ridge, hidden in the ocean off the coast. The two sides of the San Andreas Fault slip past each other rather than pulling apart. Wilson suggested that perhaps the San Andreas Fault is one of those offsetting *transform faults*. To the south, the spreading of the fault had opened up the Gulf of California. To the north, the spreading center of the San Juan de Fuca Ridge lay buried in mud on the seafloor.

Building on Tuzo's theories, geophysicist Tanya Atwater worked out the zebra-stripe pattern of magnetic stripes on the bottom of the ocean along the San Juan de Fuca Ridge. When she published her reconstruction of plate movements based on those magnetic measurements, it proved the key event in confirming the theory of plate tectonics for many scientists. Atwater and her colleagues concluded that three different plates collided here, forming a "triple junction" between the giant Pacific and North American Plates, with a small Farallon Plate caught in the crunch. The larger plate with the light rock of North America embedded on top drove the Farallon Plate deep beneath the surface. Since the rocks of the now subducted plate had lots of water in their structure, the extreme heat turned this water into superheated steam as the plate descended towards the semimolten rock of the mantle perhaps 50 miles (80 km) below the surface. This remelted crustal plate with its volatile burden of trapped, heated water provided the energy for the chain of massive volcanoes that built the Cascades and the Aleutian Islands, strung out off the coast of Alaska.

Mount Kilimanjaro

Africa

The tallest mountain in Africa has long astonished human beings who turned to stare at its gleaming, glacier-topped peaks covered permanently with ice just 200 miles (320 km) south of the equator. The people who lived at its base called it "shining mountain" and told fearful stories of the strange substance that covered its peak and doomed anyone who entered there. The idea of a snow-covered mountain close by the equator was such a remote and implausible tale that the ancient Greeks mentioned it with a tinge of myth and when the first Europeans reported spotted its gleaming summit, they were ridiculed and dismissed.

When indisputable evidence of the existence of the 19,340-foot (5,900-m) peak sheathed in a cap of year-round glaciers did finally seep out into the wider world, it was a sensation—a land of great glaciers, twisted ice sculptures, strange plants, lush rain forests, bizarre storms, and everything from elephants to leopards frozen into the ice. That was then.

Now, for the first time in 11,000 years, the snows of Kilimanjaro have melted and many experts believe the last of its glaciers will vanish within the decade—thanks to a combination of global warming and the impact of the burning and cutting of vast swaths of rain forest at the foot of the great mountain. (See upper color insert on page C-7.) Climate experts are still debating what has caused the loss of Kilimanjaro's ancient ice cap. Many say it is a symptom of the pollution-spurred warming of the atmosphere. Others point to the impact on local rainfall caused by the clearing of huge stands of forest, often as a result of the use of fire by desperately poor local people who smoke out bees from their hives so they can collect the honey. Either way, the startling change in the glaciers of Kilimanjaro offers a sobering illustration of the impact of human beings on even something so vast as the climate of the planet.

THE SHINING MOUNTAIN

Kilimanjaro, whose name is derived from the Swahili word for "Shining Mountain," is the merger of three different *volcanoes* into a single, massive stratovolcano, considered the largest freestanding volcano in the world—if you do not count Mauna Kea where you must measure from the seafloor to the summit. Two of the volcanoes that have built the mountain are considered extinct. The oldest, Shira, has not erupted in 500,000 years. The next oldest, Mawenzi, continued to erupt for another 40,000 years before it too fell silent. But at about that same time, the youngest and now tallest of the three volcanic peaks began to erupt. Kibo built its summit to an estimated 19,400 feet (5,900 m) in a series of eruptions during the next 200,000 years, before settling into a semidormant state. The summit is now crowned with a huge crater. Vents inside the crater erupted as recently as 200 years ago. The air inside the crater still smells of sulfur and the ground remains

The rapidly melting glaciers of Mount Kilimanjaro are dwarfed by Lambert Glacier in Antarctica, the world's largest. The focal point of this satellite image is an icefall that feeds into the glacier from the polar ice sheet. Ice flows like water, albeit much more slowly. Cracks can be seen in this icefall as it bends and twists on its slow-motion descent 1,300 feet (400 m) to the glacier below. *(NASA and USGS)*

hot to the touch, so geologists warn that the great mountain could some day resume its career as an active volcano.

But it is the startling near-disappearance of Kilimanjaro's once massive glacial cap in recent decades that has riveted the attention of geologists and climate specialists worldwide; the depletion of the glacier is one of the most visible and unsettling possible symptoms of the warming of the planet as a result of the massive amount of carbon dioxide from the burning of fossil fuel released into the atmosphere during the 20th century. Although climate experts continue to debate the relative contributions of deforestation and global warming, the changes have been used as a case study in climate change at scientific conferences on global warming.

The mountain's year-round ice cap has long been its most distinctive feature, although the mountain has long remained hidden in the great wilderness of Africa's interior. Although scattered written references to a great, white mountain in Africa date back at least 1,800 years, the first European to see the mountain and record his impressions was Johannes Rebmann, a Swiss-German missionary who journeyed across Africa as he struggled to save souls and spread the Gospel. In April 1848, a local caravan guide led the missionary within sight of the gleaming summit. He recorded his impression in volume I of the *Church Missionary Intelligencer* in May 1849:

> I observed something remarkably white on the top of a high mountain, and first supposed that it was a very white cloud, in which supposition my guide also confirmed me, but having gone a few paces more I could no more rest satisfied with that explanation; and while I was asking my guide a second time whether that white thing was indeed a cloud and scarcely listening to his answer that yonder was a cloud but what that white was he did not know, but supposed it was coldness—the most delightful recognition took place in my mind, of an old well-known European guest called snow. All the strange stories we had so often heard about the gold and silver mountain Kilimanjaro, supposed to be inaccessible on account of evil spirits, which had killed a great many of those who had attempted to ascend it, were now at once rendered intelligible to me, as the extreme cold, to which poor Natives are perfect strangers, would soon chill and kill the half-naked visitors. . . . The cold temperature of the higher regions constituted a limit beyond which they dared not venture. This had prevented them from exploring it, and left them in utter ignorance of such a thing as "snow," although not in ignorance of that which they so greatly dreaded—"coldness."

However, the glaciers that made Kilimanjaro so strange and awe-inspiring even from a great distance have shrunk by an estimated 82 percent since 1912. Many geologists believe the last vestiges of these

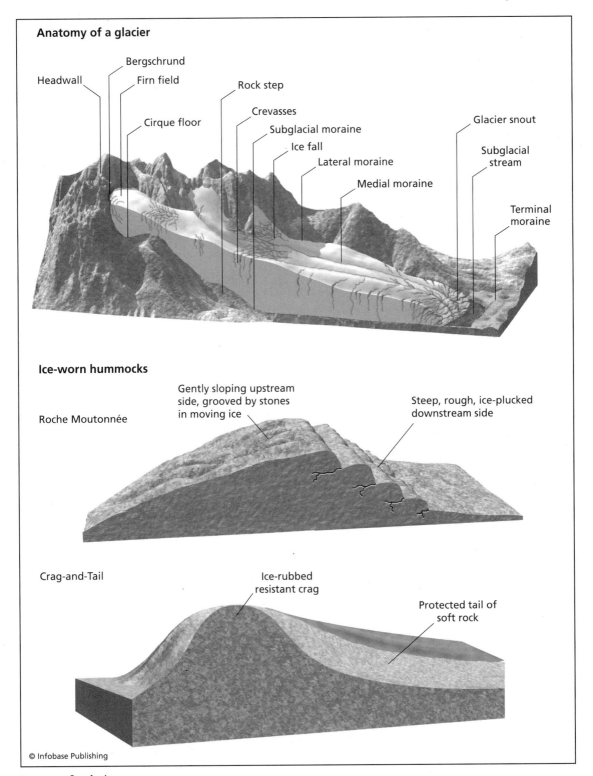

Anatomy of a glacier

Headwall

Bergschrund

Firn field

Cirque floor

Rock step

Crevasses

Subglacial moraine

Ice fall

Lateral moraine

Medial moraine

Glacier snout

Subglacial stream

Terminal moraine

Ice-worn hummocks

Roche Moutonnée

Gently sloping upstream side, grooved by stones in moving ice

Steep, rough, ice-plucked downstream side

Crag-and-Tail

Ice-rubbed resistant crag

Protected tail of soft rock

© Infobase Publishing

Features of a glacier

tropical glaciers will vanish in the next 15 years. If that happens, the summit of the mountain will be ice-free for the first time in nearly 12,000 years. The reported retreat of the Kilimanjaro glaciers is perhaps the most dramatic example of a global trend. In fact, glaciers have retreated dramatically in the Himalayas, the Alps, the Rocky Mountains, the Cascade Range, the southern Andes and isolated tropical mountains like Kilimanjaro.

Of course, glaciers have long advanced and retreated with shifts in the climate—carving the face of mountains in the process. Many of the U-shaped valleys in mountain ranges throughout the world, including places like Yosemite in the Sierra Nevada of California, have been carved by glaciers that have since withdrawn. During the last ice age some 11,000 years ago, glaciers covered much of North America, including a layer of ice a mile (1.6 km) thick atop present-day Chicago, which carved out the basins of the Great Lakes. But the accelerated retreat of glaciers throughout the world on peaks like Kilimanjaro in the past 20 years has alarmed many climate experts.

Glaciers form in regions when the summer sun cannot melt away the winter's accumulation of snow. As excess snow builds up winter after winter, it is compressed to create a great mass of hard, compressed ice that forms a glacier. All glaciers exist in a delicate balance based on its mass, melting, evaporation, and the slope of the valley in which the glacier rests. If enough snow accumulates to compress additional layers of ice, the glacier will advance down the valley—grinding up even hard rocks as it advances. On the other hand, if the rocks on which the glacier rests pick up too much heat, they will melt the base of the glacier. This causes overlying layers to break off. In that case, the glacier will retreat, melting and reducing its extent as the leading wall of ice crumbles and disappears. In this way, a melting glacier looks like it is receding uphill.

GLACIERS IN FULL RETREAT

The great majority of the Earth's glaciers are now in full retreat, according to the World Glacier Monitoring Service. For instance, between 1995 and 2000, 103 of 110 glaciers in Switzerland, 95 of 99 glaciers in Austria, all 99 glaciers in Italy, and all six glaciers in France were in retreat. That also applies to 67 percent of the Himalayan glaciers, 95 percent of the glaciers in China, almost all of the glaciers in North America, and the great majority of the glaciers in Asia, New Zealand, and South America. Researchers from the University of Alaska estimate that Alaska may be losing 15 to 31 cubic miles (62.5–129.2 km³) of ice each year.

The demise of the glaciers that hold an estimated 8 percent of the world's freshwater in storage will have a significant impact. (See lower color insert on page C-7.) Glaciers often play a vital role in regulating runoff—storing the winter rains and snows as ice and then releasing the water slowly throughout the dry season. As a result, agricultural areas that rely on runoff from glacier-topped mountains could face severe water shortages. Moreover, streams fed by glacial runoff also generate a significant amount of *hydroelectric* power. Pakistan depends heavily on glacial runoff from the high, cold mountains that occupy much of its territory. One of the reasons Pakistan is struggling with India for control of the Kashmir area is that this region has many glaciers, resulting in much hydroelectric power. Many plants and animals have also adapted to the influence of glaciers on local weather patterns and runoff. Species of fish like salmon and cutthroat trout migrate up these glacially fed rivers and depend on the chilled water in high mountain streams and lakes for crucial aspects of their life cycle.

Finally, the Earth's glaciers keep a significant amount of water in storage that would otherwise flow into the ocean—raising sea levels worldwide. If the 24,000 cubic miles (100,032 km³) of ice stored in the world's mountain glaciers were to melt, it would raise sea level by 18 inches (46 cm), according to estimates by Lonnie Thompson, a senior research scientist at Ohio State University's Byrd Polar Research Center. Such a sea level rise would flood the homes of an estimated 100 million people in Bangladesh alone. Of course, that is nothing compared to the impact of any meltdown of the ice caps. If the ice covering the Antarctic melted, it would raise sea levels by a cataclysmic 230 feet (70 m). However, while a South Pole meltdown remains unlikely, the mountain glaciers are already melting fast.

On Kilimanjaro, the 300-foot-thick (90-m) layer of ice has nearly vanished. In a 14-year period from 1984 to 1998, one carefully measured glacier there receded 980 feet (300 m). The Furtwängler Glacier shrank from an area of 1,216,320 square feet (113,000 m²) to 645,840 square feet (60,000 m²) between 1976 and 2000. On average, the glaciers thin by about 18 inches (46 cm) each year, but even that rapid loss may accelerate. Scientists measuring the Furtwängler Glacier in 2006 discovered a hole in the center, which extended some 20 feet (6 m) down to the bedrock. This melt hole will probably split the glacier in two, which could lead to its rapid breakup.

Nearby Mount Kenya, an extinct volcano that was once higher than Kilimanjaro, is in a similar state, having lost at least 45 percent of its glacial mass in the past 50 years. The U.S. Geological Survey counted 18 glaciers on Mount Kenya in 1900, but by 1986 only 11 remained. The total area covered by glaciers on that mountain declined from 0.62 square miles (1.6 km²) to 0.15 square miles (0.4 km²).

The loss of the glaciers on top of Kilimanjaro will affect the entire region. Currently, the mountain creates its own weather system, which

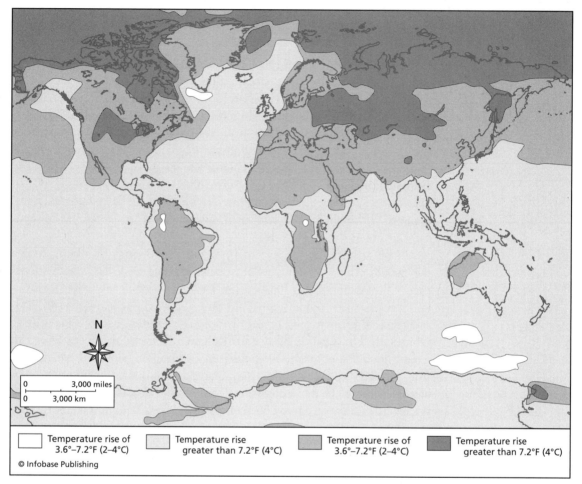

| | Temperature rise of 3.6°–7.2°F (2–4°C) | | Temperature rise greater than 7.2°F (4°C) | | Temperature rise of 3.6°–7.2°F (2–4°C) | | Temperature rise greater than 7.2°F (4°C) |

© Infobase Publishing

Projection of future average surface temperature increases based on a rise in atmospheric carbon dioxide of 1 percent per year. The scenario depicted is the outcome of the atmospheric carbon dioxide level doubling in 70 years.

affects virtually every plant and animal. The mountain itself has six major climate zones along its 19,000-foot (5,790-m) height, including cultivated farmland at its base, thick rain forests with six or seven feet (1.8–2 m) of rainfall each year, heath, moorland, alpine desert, and the frozen glacial terrain of the summit. The great mass of the mountain lies close to both the heated semidesert of the *Great Rift Valley* and the warm, wet tropical forests of eastern Africa. As a result, moisture-laden air rises up the flanks of the mountain from the tropics. As this warm, wet tropical air rises, it cools and the moisture condenses. This waters the midmountain tropical forest, with its palms, hanging mosses, 13-foot (4-m)-tall camphorwood trees, and diverse animals like the blue and Colobus monkeys, leopards, elephants, buffalo, giraffes, and lions.

MOUNTAIN MAKES ITS OWN WEATHER

The mountain enjoys two distinct rainy seasons, one from March through June and the other during November and December, although rainfall varies dramatically from one elevation to the next. Most of the rain falls in the forested zone, with much less making it to the upper reaches of the mountain. The rain that falls in the forested region feeds streams and springs that provide most of the water for more than 1 million people in

KILIMANJARO LIFE ZONES

- ✦ Summit (16,500 to 19340 feet [5,030–5,900 m]): This near-Arctic environment exists just 220 miles (350 km) from the equator, with oxygen levels half those found at sea level. Although a frozen leopard was found near the crater at the summit in 1926, few animals venture into this zone and the plants are limited to a few tough species of lichen.
- ✦ Alpine Desert (13,200 to 16,500 feet [4,020–5,030 m]): This harsh zone has little rainfall and few plants, in part because of temperature swings that can vary from below freezing to 100°F (38°C) in a single day. The thin soil supports only a few tough grasses, and the strange moss ball which envelops bits of soil then blows about in the wind, totally self-contained.
- ✦ Moorland (11,000 to 13,200 feet [3,350–4,020 m]): Kilimanjaro's most distinctive and endangered plants grow in this zone, with its limited rain and intermittent frost. The vegetation includes a unique species of Lobelia, an annual flowering plant used as a traditional treatment for respiratory and muscle disorders and in modern medicines to treat asthma, food poisoning, and nicotine addiction. The mountain also harbors a giant species of senecios, giant, otherwordly *succulents* that grow on wood stems and cope with drought with pulpy leaf rosettes that store moisture and close at night to protect against frost. Birds of prey like the crowned eagle and lammergeyer patrol the skies and elands, duikers, African hunting dogs, and sometimes even elephants pass through on occasion.
- ✦ Heath (9,200 to 11,000 feet [2,800–3,350 m]): This zone is often swathed in mist and fog rising out of the rain forest below. The terrain is marked by an array of grasses and many flowers, including the artichoke-like protea and a tall, colorful red or yellow-blossomed plant know as the red-hot poker.
- ✦ Rain Forest (6,000 to 9,200 feet [1,830–2,800 m]): This thick forest zone gets an average of 6.5 feet (2 m) of rain every year, which supports a riot of plants like sycamore figs, palms, and massive camphorwood trees. Some seven species of primates live in the forest and many of the species of antelope found on the mountain, as well as leopards, elephants, buffalo, and giraffes.
- ✦ Cultivated Zone (2,600 to 6,000 feet [790–1,830 m]): The soil laced with Kilimanjaro's volcanic ash holds moisture well, providing fertile land for agriculture. Farmland growing mostly bananas and coffee has largely replaced the lowland forests and driven off much of the wildlife. However, night dwellers like the galagos, a lemurlike creature, and the furry, screeching tree hyrax still come out at night.

the mountain's watershed. The forested belt also accounts for the greatest variety of plant and animal species. Some 900 plant species grow in the forested zone, compared to 1,600 on the rest of the mountain. Moreover, the mountain has 140 known species of mammals, including 87 species that live only in the forested area. The black rhinoceros, reedbuck, and klipspringer have all gone extinct on the mountain, but its slopes still harbor 24 species of antelope, 25 species of meateaters, 7 species of primates, and 25 species of bats.

GREAT RIFT VALLEY SHAPES CONTINENT

Kilimanjaro's violent creation also sheds light on the evolution of the whole surface of the planet, since it was created as a direct result of the jostling of crustal plates and lies along one of the most interesting and important geological features on the surface of the planet. Africa's Great Rift Valley runs close by Kilimanjaro and accounts for its creation, along with a chain of other extinct volcanoes including Mount Kenya, Africa's second highest peak. In effect, the collision of two great crustal plates first uplifted a portion of Africa, then shifted and pulled apart along a great sunken valley running from the Red Sea in the Middle East down through East Africa. Although Kilimanjaro rises alongside this rift in the earth's crust, the tectonic forces that caused the rift also fed magma into the fissures in the earth beneath Africa's tallest mountain. In fact, the Red Sea and the Great Rift Valley now stand in the spreading gap between two continental plates. Movement along this fissure will likely split East Africa off the continent and move it off to the east, where it will become an island continent like Australia. In another 200 million years, an ocean as broad as the Atlantic may separate East Africa from the rest of its erstwhile continent. By then Kilimanjaro will have likely been eroded down to gravel and stone.

The fissure that created the Great Rift Valley began to open in Northern Africa some 35 million years ago, opening up along the long, straight line of the 1,600-mile (2,560-km) long Red Sea. The widening gap split Arabia off the African continent. The crack that created the Red Sea and the Great Rift Valley also runs through the Gulf of Aqaba. Geologists think that the fissure emerging under the Red Sea and the valley will split into a system of ridges dividing at least three different crustal plates. That will eventually create an ocean ridge running down Africa's Great Rift Valley. However, other geologists suspect shifts by other plates will instead seal up this third arm of the rift before it opens.

The nearly 4,000-mile-long (6,400-km) rift system remains complex and poorly understood. Some sections are splitting apart. Other sections are instead transform faults, sideways cracks like San Andreas Fault in

California that offset a long-running fissure between two colliding plates. The entire system starts near Syria then runs down the Jordan River, along the Sea of Galilee, through the Dead Sea, and finally to the Red Sea before continuing on down to Africa. The portions of the system along this stretch are offsetting transform faults. The actual crack does not start rifting until well down into Africa, where the plate edges create two rift systems. The rifted slump in the crust is marked in Africa by a series of mountains, including Kilimanjaro. The rift also has created deep troughs filled with some of the world's largest freshwater lakes. Several plateaus divide the two rift systems, and here titanic geological forces have created 4,500-foot-deep (1,390-m) Lake Tanganyika, and Lake Victoria, the second largest freshwater lake in the world.

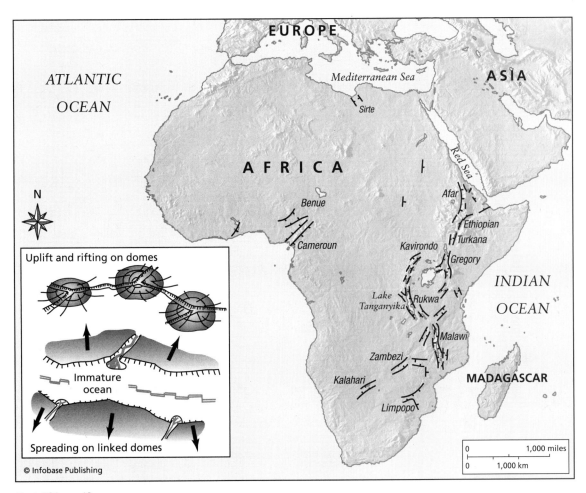

East African rift

The human species appears to have first emerged in this Rift Valley, perhaps within sight of the ice-covered peaks of Kilimanjaro. Geneticists, comparing the *DNA* blueprint of all major racial groups living today, can calculate how closely related one group is to another and how long it has been since they shared a common ancestor. This is because in between the roughly 30,000 genes a certain amount of random DNA junk accumulates. Since these noncoding DNA pieces do not actually do anything, they are passed along without being modified by the mutations and adaptations of the functional genes. Therefore, geneticists can compare these noncoding DNA "introns" from one species to another. Such studies in human beings suggest that the first human beings lived in Africa between about 80,000 and 180,000 years ago.

Moreover, *paleontologists* have discovered a fascinating set of fossilized bones of the earliest human ancestors in the Great Rift Valley, not far from Kilimanjaro. In Olduvai Gorge just northwest of Kilimanjaro, scientists found the 3 to 4 million-year-old skeleton of "Lucy," one of the earliest human ancestors. Experts on human evolution now believe that several contending species of small, upright-walking, big-brained humanoids lived in the forests and savannas of East Africa. They spread outward across the other continents from there, probably in several waves. Modern *homo sapiens*, the descendents of Lucy and her kind, then spread outward from Africa.

Ever since, explorers and settlers have been rediscovering the great mountain, starting with the mysterious people who left their stone bowls on the mountain's lower slopes at least 3,000 years ago. Roughly 1,800 years ago, the great Greek astronomer and mapmaker Ptolemy of Alexandria wrote of a "great snow mountain" in East Africa, deep in the territory of people he described as cannibals. This is the earliest known written record of Kilimanjaro. Not another word appears in the written record for 1,000 years, when the 13th-century Arab geographer Abd'l Fida wrote of a mountain that was "white in color." All that while, people were living on the mountain and taking advantage of its rich array of plants and animals. Many different groups apparently settled there prior to about 500 years ago, including groups of forest-dwelling pygmies and herders who lived on the plains.

About 400 years ago, a group called the Chagga moved into the area and drove out or absorbed the previous residents. The Chagga's social and political structure was based on hundreds of tribelike clans, which spent much of their time in generally nonviolent raids on one another. They often took slaves from rival clans, burnt down one another's villages and stole one another's livestock, but usually avoided bloodshed since smaller groups usually simply ran away when confronted by a superior force.

AGE OF EXPLORATION

Although various European explorers undertook expeditions that criss-crossed Africa, a daring pair of missionaries were the first non-natives to record seeing the gleaming summit of Kilimanjaro. One was Ludwig Krapf (1810–81), a German missionary who came to East Africa to save souls, but instead lost his wife and child and nearly his own life to malaria. As he recovered, he translated the Bible into Swahili and hatched a plan to walk the width of Africa to lay the groundwork for a chain of missions. But after 14 years of difficult and exhausting work, he had made just seven converts.

So with the help of Johannes Rebmann (1820–76), Krapf resolved to set out for unknown territory, where he hoped the locals might prove more convertible. In 1848, with an Arab caravan leader for a guide and eight natives to carry their supplies, they set out to find a rumored mountain protected by evil spirits and crowned with a strange white substance resembling silver that the locals called "cold." Rebmann made an exploratory trip and came within sight of Kilimanjaro. But when he sent word of his discovery back to Germany, most experts dismissed the report, concluding it was impossible for a mountain to maintain a snow cover so close to the equator—although it was well known that the snow-covered Andes crossed the equator in South America.

However, subsequent expeditions confirmed the missionary's report. In the course of the next 60 years, repeated efforts to reach the summit ended in failure, largely due to the difficulty of hauling supplies through the roadless jungles and grasslands for weeks just to reach the base of the mountain. The efforts were also complicated by warfare, rebellion, and political instability as Britain and Germany contended for economic dominance of East Africa, partly by stirring up warfare involving their various native allies. Germany and Britain eventually divided the region into their different spheres, with Germany attempting to colonize the area around Kilimanjaro.

In the end, it took near-fanatical persistence and great organizational skills to reach the summit for the first time. Dr. Hans Meyer (1858–1929) made three attempts to reach the top, most of them ending in danger, frustration, and failure. A geology professor and son of a wealthy German editor, Meyer reached the 18,000-foot (5,400-m) mark on his first attempt. On his second try, he ran into an Arab-led revolt against the Germans and was captured by the rebels. He was held prisoner until his father paid a 10,000-rupee ransom. That would have discouraged most men, but Meyer simply waited for the Germans to suppress the rebellion, then returned for his third attempt. This time, he established a series of base camps on the approach to the mountain. He then arranged for porters to supply the base camps with food and supplies. These base

MOUNT KENYA

Once, Mount Kenya rose much higher than the upstart Kilimanjaro, driven by the same volcanic cataclysm unleashed by the clashing of continents that formed the Great Rift Valley. But Mount Kenya stopped erupting at least 2.6 million years ago and the inexorable hand of erosion, coupled with the slumping of the crust under the extinct volcano's great weight, has reduced its height to 17,060 feet (5,200 m). Located in central Kenya some 100 miles (160 km) southeast of Nairobi, the great mountain's slopes nurture a shifting terrain of different life zones. Unlike Kilimanjaro, Mount Kenya has a thick forest of bamboo at about the 7,500 feet (2,500 m) elevation, and a higher elevation forest of small, twisted trees thickly hung with "goat's beard" lichen. The mountain also lacks Kilimanjaro's massive cap of year-round glaciers, since its 12 small existing glaciers are rapidly dwindling. Gaining the summit of Mount Kenya does require ropes and technical climbing skill, unlike Kilimanjaro, which is the world's tallest mountain whose summit is accessible to mere hikers. The first recorded ascent to the highest point on the mountain was in 1929, a climb by Eric Shipton and Bill Tilman. However, in the end even proud Kilimanjaro will lose its snowy glaciers, according to climate scientists. Small comfort for Mount Kenya—Kilimanjaro will still be taller.

camps allowed him to make repeated approaches to the summit without having to return all the way to the foot of the mountain.

That proved the winning strategy. In 1889, Meyer assembled a major expedition that included climber Herr Ludwig Purtscheller, two local chiefs, nine porters, three other native supervisors, one cook, and one guide. Goaded on by Meyer's penchant for flogging anyone who committed even a minor breach of discipline, the expedition proceeded despite desertions, the lack of a trail, dangerous elephant pits dug and concealed by the locals, and the intermittent hostility of the local tribes.

They struggled up a mountain that had much more snow and much more extensive and difficult glaciers than the mountain has today. On one push for the summit, they spent all their time, energy, and supplies using ice picks to hack out a set of steps up an otherwise unclimbable portion of a glacier. Exhausted, they made their way back to the base camp in the dark, rested and made another attempt that took advantage of their laboriously carved glacier steps.

Finally, on October 6, 1889, they stood on top of the highest point in Africa, little knowing that at that moment they could see more square miles of land than from any other place on the planet, since Kilimanjaro rises alone from the middle of a great lowland, with no other mountains to block the view to the horizon. The ascent was a triumph of persistence, organization, and daring. For many decades after Meyer's climb, only a handful of other people struggled to Africa's highest point. Of course, that has all changed now.

Today, Kilimanjaro is one of the Seven Summits, the high points of each continent. Moreover, the three to seven day ascent requires no technical climbing skills and Kilimanjaro remains the only one of the Seven Summits that can be surmounted with no gear more technical than a walking stick. As a result, some 35,000 people climb the peak every year. Of course, they do not have to hack steps out of the glaciers anymore. And soon enough, they will not have any glaciers to look at. And so they will never see the mountain that Ernest Hemingway once described as "wide as all the world, great, high, and unbelievably white in the Sun."

Humphreys Peak

Arizona, North America

The Magician watched the steaming, glowing lava rolling slowly and inexorably towards him, down the splintered and devastated slopes of the mountains that had sustained his people since the days of myth. He wore the adornments of his station, the intricate turquoise jewelry, the shells, and the carved wand, all decorated with stones and feathers carried along thousand-mile-long trade routes connecting the diverse and thriving civilizations spread throughout the American Southwest 1,000 years ago.

Praying and chanting, he lay down a row of corn—an offering to the advancing wall of lava that now threatened to scatter his people across an unforgiving world, despite all their reverence and care. Many people had already fled the area over the years in which the ground had shaken and trembled. But the Magician and his followers had waited, wondering at the plan of the gods to shake the earth so capriciously.

But then the shaking Earth had produced great, yawning cracks that emitted steam and smoke. These fissures, in turn, had given way to terrifying explosions, so that molten rocks and ash blasted out of sudden holes in the earth. The people knew that great forces lived down there in the Earth. After all, they had long left their offerings at the mouths of the blowholes—cracks that half the year breathed in and half the year expelled the breath of the earth so forcefully that eagle feathers could dance on the musty, earth-smelling updraft. Now, those Earth spirits threw out great boulders, which fell with devastating effect.

Finally, the molten rock had come up out of the Earth, thick as wet cornmeal, oozing up out of the conical mountains of ash the previous explosions had built. The lava came up out of the earth and set about hunting for any living thing. The low, terrible flow of rock spread out from the cinder cones in rivers of stone, incinerating everything in its path.

So now the Magician came with his people watching, to make a final offering to the lava, which had claimed all their villages and their crops and the open meadows that they had farmed for uncounted generations. He did not expect the row of corn to stop the molten rock, which had its own mind and purpose. He offered it in reverence and respect, that the Earth spirits might have pity on them and let them go their way. The Magician stepped back and the lava flowed over the ears of corn, without stopping. So the Magician and all his people turned away from the lava and went on out into that strange world, transformed so utterly by the inexplicable and implacable fury of the Earth.

BUILDING A MOUNTAIN, ONE ERUPTION AT A TIME

Countless such scenes no doubt attended the most recent volcanic outpouring in the 8-million-year process of building Humphreys Peak, the tallest mountain in Arizona. Archeologists have unearthed the ash-smothered villages, the lava-created casts of the corn placed carefully in the lava's path, and even the richly decorated burial site of the headman or shaman they have dubbed the "Magician," because of the elaborately carved, turquoise-inlaid wands buried with him.

At 12,630 feet (3,850 m), Humphreys Peak gains less than half the altitude of the world's highest peaks, but it offers a compelling story about the long, complex relationship between human beings and mountains and a complex revelation of the impact of geology and mountain-building processes on living things. (See upper color insert on page C-8.) The comparatively young mountain was built up as a result of volcanic cataclysms, including the most recent outpouring in 1064–65, which had a dramatic effect on existing civilizations and which left the raw, colorful landscape of Sunset Crater National Monument.

The massive San Francisco Mountains volcanic field sits on the southern edge of the Colorado Plateau, a region of massive uplift—driven by the jostling of crustal plates. Geologists believe deep currents in the molten earth drove the movement of the hard, cold crustal plates and the uplift of the western one-third of the continental United States. These forces drove the rise of the Rocky Mountains, the spectacular downcutting of the Grand Canyon, and the outburst of volcanic activity around present-day Flagstaff, Arizona.

Geologists have counted some 600 different volcanoes in a field of peaks, flows, and cinder cones that covers much of north-central Arizona, from the Little Colorado River west to Ash Fork and from Cameron down to the 1,000-foot (300-m)-high line of cliffs dubbed the *Mogollon Rim*, which is the southern edge of the Colorado Plateau. Geologists have labored to date the complex layers of lava and array of *cinder cones* and volcanoes, trying to piece together the titanic sequence of events. Mostly, they have relied on chemical analysis of radioactive elements in the rock, which are set into place when the molten rock hardens and then decay at a steady rate. Those analyses indicate that the oldest volcanic rocks in the field date back some 8 million years and that major eruptions took place every 13,000 years or so. Even if half of the volcanic outbursts have been buried, the time between major eruptions still stands at about 7,000 years—a blink of an eye in geological time. Since the last major outburst was 1,000 years ago, the still active volcanic field may remain completely quiet for another 6,000 years—which was the time it took human beings to progress from the invention of the first crude system of writing to landing on the Moon.

Geologists are still trying to understand the 8-million-year sequence of eruptions that built Humphreys Peak and the surrounding volcanic landscape. Apparently, a seemingly inexhaustible reservoir of basalt lies miles beneath the surface, pooling in some flaw of the Earth and rising periodically when the cold, hard rock overhead cracks from the strain of the molten rock pressing up from below. The earliest eruptions took place southwest of Flagstaff near the present-day Mogollon Rim. The first molten rock that gushed to the surface along fissures and volcanoes closely resembled the dark, iron-rich, nonexplosive, thick lavas that have built Hawaii out in the Pacific. For reasons geologists still do not entirely understand, the eruptions gradually migrated towards the northeast.

Starting some 4 million years ago, a different chemical composition of lava began to erupt in volcanic centers located along major breaks in the Earth's crust. The earlier eruptions were comprised of basalt, similar in composition to the oceanic crust. But the new eruptions shifted to lavas with a composition closer to granite, including andesite, dacite, and *rhyolite*. These formed thick, stubby flows that quickly built tall, steep-sided mountains over the vents from which the lava issued. The andesite and dacite lavas built up the present-day Bill Williams Mountain starting about 4 million years ago. As the center of the eruptions continued to shift in the course of the next 1.5 million years, they created Sitgreaves Mountain and then Kendrick Peak, all fed from the same deep, vast reservoir of lava.

The construction of Humphreys Peak itself began when the center of the eruptions jumped eastward to a parallel fracture system. One eruption followed another at intervals of 7,000 to 15,000 years until the lava had built a massive, cone-shaped mountain by about 400,000 years ago. The alternating layers of viscous, slow-flowing lava and cinders constructed a classic, cone-shaped composite volcano, illuminated by geysers of lava and billowing clouds of ash. Although Humphreys Peak is considered a very young mountain, when it was built the ancestors of human beings consisted of a few small, struggling bands living somewhere in southern Africa. Anthropologists and geneticists who have analyzed DNA patterns in modern humans calculate that Homo sapiens spread out of Africa as recently as 100,000 years ago. Evidence suggests that the first humans arrived in North America between 15,000 and 40,000 years ago. So the cataclysm of volcanoes that built Humphreys Peak had no human witness.

The eruptions built classic, cone-shaped peaks, like the modern Cascades range that includes Mount Saint Helens. At the base of the mountain, thick, pasty lava piled up to create interlocking lava domes and subsidiary peaks, like Elden Mountain. Sometime between 200,000 and 400,000 years ago, events reached a titanic climax. At that point, the mountain towered into a single cone some 15,000 feet (4,570 m) tall. Then, most likely, earthquakes triggered a massive series of landslides that shaved off one side of the mountain. This event probably released the massive reservoir of lava and superheated steam in the throat of the volcano. Instead of spewing out the top, much of the rock and ash blasted out sideways—tearing open the mountain, much as Mount Saint Helens exploded in more recent times. As a result, the eruption decapitated the mountain—blowing off the top 3,000 feet (910 m) of rock and leaving a massive hole in the center of the mountain, today dubbed the Inner Basin. Debris from the explosion and landslide settled all around the mountain, leaving the Inner Basin surrounded by towering cliffs.

SUNSET CRATER PHASE

After that, the center of the eruptions shifted again, this time towards what would become Sunset Crater. In the meantime, the planet wobbled in its orbit around the Sun, creating just enough change in solar energy to usher in periodic ice ages. In these periods of intense cold lasting for thousands of years, glaciers formed in the Inner Basin, gouging out the surrounding cliffs and *pulverizing* the floor of the basin. The glaciers left layers of crushed rock that would later create a perfect underground storage area for snow and ice melting from the surrounding peaks. That stored underground water in a natural aquifer today supplies the city of Flagstaff with all its drinking water, yet another example of the close dependence of human beings on the accidents of geology.

Humphreys Peak fell largely silent after this violent climax, now sculpted by rain and ice instead of the furies of the Earth. The locus of the volcanic activity shifted north and east, creating a bizarre landscape of vents and cinder cones, none of which rose to challenge the great mass of Humphreys Peak. The landscape around Humphreys offers a vivid illustration of volcanic forms. The older cinder cones have eroded to low mounds while the younger ones retain their steep, smooth sides, topped by well-formed craters. Many of the cinder cones appear randomly scattered about, their location dictated by the hidden logic of cracks deep beneath the surface. Superheated, pressurized lava moved along this network of fissures and found its way to the surface from great reservoirs of molten stone 35 to 50 miles (56–80 km) beneath the surface.

The most recent episode in this complex mountain-building project came in the late fall or winter of 1064-65 C.E., about the time the Normans crossed the English Channel to conquer England. At that time, a farm-based civilization had spread throughout the American Southwest, composed of a variety of distinctive cultures linked by sprawling trade routes that stretched from the coast of California into New Mexico and from the San Francisco Peaks deep into the complex civilizations of Meso-America.

Archeologists have named the people living in the region around Humphreys Peak the Sinagua, taking the name from the Spanish term for the mountains—Sierra Sinagua, which means "mountains without water." The Sinagua occupied a middle ground between the Anasazi of ancestral Puebloans living in the Colorado Plateau to the north and the Hohokam, who lived along the flood-prone rivers of the lower desert regions. The Sinagua first settled in the area in about 600 C.E., establishing small villages sheltering extended family units across a semiarid area of about 3,100 square miles (8,030 km²). Settled in a transitional area between the more urbanized, populous civilizations to the north and south, the Sinagua benefited from living along a major trade route and borrowed traditions from the other cultures.

Lacking reliable rivers and depending on fitful streams and springs, the Sinagua in the early years of their long occupation of the high, cold, volcanic lands around Humphreys Peak lived in the relatively fertile transitional areas between the upper elevation ponderosa pine forests and the piñon juniper woodlands. This ecological transition zone was sprinkled with open, grassy, parklike areas with well-developed soil that would hold moisture longer than that in the surrounding woodlands. The Sinagua lived in small groups and pithouses near these grassy parks, surrounded by the rocky landscape. They took full advantage of the ecological variety of the area, planting mostly rain-watered crops in the few good growing areas and moving from piñons to pines and then on up the mountain into the forests of spruce, aspen, and firs at the higher elevations. Mountains have long provided such bounty to hunters and gatherers, enabling people to harvest a variety of resources simply by changing elevations with the shift in the seasons.

The Sinagua excavated pit houses, some of them 25 feet (8 m) in diameter, big enough to hold ceremonies and gatherings for many people. Most of the settlements had three to 10 smaller pit houses, dug into the ground with a domelike door fashioned from logs and saplings plastered over with mud. They also constructed great, walled ball courts, perhaps borrowed from similar structures in the much more urban civilizations in Mexico such as the Maya. Archeologists believe they staged ritual games and ceremonies in the ball courts, perhaps attended by people from surrounding villages. The renewed onset of volcanic eruptions from perhaps 1064 to 1250 had dramatic effects on this inventive and adaptable civilization.

Most directly affected were some 50 villages close to the site of the first series of eruptions. Many moved as an increase in the number of earthquakes laid the groundwork for the renewed volcanism. Archeologists have found evidence that people laboriously took apart their pit houses and used the precious and laboriously cut logs to build new villages further from the area most affected by the ground tremors. They were the lucky ones. When the eruptions finally came, the impact in the immediate area was devastating. The explosions and ashfall exterminated all vegetation within a two-mile (3.2-km) radius of the cinder cone, now known as Sunset Crater for the fiery red cast of its cinders. The ash, fire, poisonous gases and acidic rains probably debilitated almost all the plant growth within about 15 miles (24 km). The growth rings of trees show that the rain of ash and acid affected tree growth throughout the region for many years.

Lava forced its way to the surface along a six-mile (10-km)-long fissure, first in geysers of steam, then in fountains of lava. Bubbles in the lava would have expanded explosively as the molten rock reached the surface, blasting open the vents and fissures and spewing the jagged, froth of glowing stone high into the atmosphere. Cooling as it rose, the fragments turned into cinders and ash. Larger masses of lava shot into the air, cooled into spherical blobs, then crashed back down to Earth as *lava bombs* of terrible destructive force. A broiling column of cinders and gas probably rose thousands of feet into the atmosphere, generating a terrifying play of lightning within the cloud of ash and making a howling roar. As the heated column of air and ash rose, it would have created a suction that would have drawn air in at the base, creating a holocaust that would have destroyed anyone foolish enough to have lingered in the area. Gradually the howling column built the cinder cone of Sunset Crater, a towering, roiling column of black smoke by day and a pillar of fire by night, attended by glowing lava bombs hurled in every direction.

Prevailing winds blew much of the ash to the east, covering some 800 square miles (2,070 km²) in a smothering blanket of ash, including the fields of hundreds of scattered villages and reaching as far as the current Hopi mesas. The lava and ash completely buried some vital Sinagua farming areas. Layers of ash clogged washes, filled ponds, and buried springs. Denuded of plants, the raw, ash-plagued soil eroded easily, altering drainages and unhinging the ecosystems that had sustained the Sinagua for generations. This terrible rain of fire and ash continued off and on for an estimated 85 years, by which time the cinder cone had grown to several hundred feet and a fine layer of ash had been spread across the region.

After the explosions had nearly subsided—although the scattering of fissures and cinder cones would continue to erupt fitfully for a total of nearly 200 years—most of the lava filled with pressurized gases had been released. Now, the lava making its way to the surface was dense and less explosive. It forced its way through the lighter cinders, breaking through the side of the cinder cone and flowing out of the base in a river of molten stone towards the drainage of the Little Colorado River. This massive, inexorable flow of black, iron-rich lava left behind a jumbled landscape of great slabs of rock and buried lava tubes, long caves created when the outer layers of a river of lava cool and harden, insulating the still molten flow inside the tube. Sometimes, this tube full of molten rock finds an outlet and the lava drains away, leaving the tube intact. Such caves can run for long distances beneath lava flows.

Now the eruptions changed character once again. As the gas escaped from the reservoir of molten rock still feeding the explosions, the outbursts grew weaker. Ejected to a much lower height, the lava bombs were still hot and sticky when they fell back to earth. They fused, forming layers of welded cinders that oozed down the side of the volcano like a lava flow. Some of these welded layers reached depths of 30 feet (9 m) and extended in mounds and clusters for a quarter mile or more from the cinder cone.

In the final phase of volcanic activity, the eruptions weakened and the lower percentage of volcanic gases in the mixture allowed more air to mix with the molten cinders and ash. The oxygen reacted with the iron in this final phase of the eruption, effectively rusting the ash red and giving the cinder cone its dramatic red hues. A few final explosions inside the cinder cone blasted out a small crater. However, most of the final flow emerged from the base of the volcano. The lava flowed through an old lava tube and emerged some five miles (8 km) from the volcano, emerging black and implacable to form a jagged landscape. The chaotic flow created a variety of lava forms, with coils, thin shells puffed up by expanding gas, blobs, and gigantic tilted slabs.

As the flow slowed and cooled, great cracks gaped open, one more than half a mile (.80 km) long. Some of the cracks were empty, but others harbor "squeeze-ups," sharp vertical grooves formed by the welling up of the stiff, thick lava that forced open the fissures. The flow includes a number of lava tubes, out of which the molten flow drained. Some are long tunnels large enough to walk through with plenty of head clearance; others form complicated branching tangles too narrow to wriggle through. One lava tube stretches for more than 230 feet (70 m). Some collect water that remains permanently frozen turning the tubes into ice caves. This violent, 200-year-long series of explosions was but a smudge compared to the much longer and more violent events that built Humphreys Peak. In fact, it produced only about one-tenth of one percent of the total lava in the San Francisco Peaks volcanic field. However, it was probably the first eruptive event to have been observed by people living in the region, and it changed their lives profoundly.

About three-fourths of the lava was converted into cinders. The cinders that fell close to the vent built Sunset Crater, a nearly perfect cone some 1,000 feet high (300 m) and one mile (1.6 km) in diameter, with a 400-foot (120-m) deep crater in the center created in the last stages of the eruptions. The rest of the lava buried nearly two square miles (5 km²) in a flow 100 feet (30 m) thick at the center, tapering off to about 10 feet (3 m) at the edges.

THE UNEXPECTED BENEFITS OF DISASTER

Undoubtedly, the explosions proved disastrous for people living in the immediate vicinity of the crater. But strangely enough, in the decades following the explosions the region underwent a major population explosion, with migrants moving in from other regions, and a blossoming of new villages—often with much more numerous and impressive structures than had existed before. What happened? How did a devastating series of volcanic explosions actually provide a long-term benefit to people living in the region? Archeologists continue to debate that very question.

Most archeologists argue that the widespread blanket of ash actually benefited farmers. They note that farmers in the high, cold, semiarid region around Humphreys Peak face two tough problems—the lack of water and the short growing season. Lacking reliable streams and rivers, the Sinagua depended heavily on fitful rainfall. Moreover, a hard early winter could cut short their growing season with fatal results. The layer of ash may have actually reduced both of those problems in many areas. The ash effectively insulated the soil, holding in both warmth and water in a combination effect that might have added weeks to the typical growing season—a vital advantage in an area where farmers struggled from one season to the next.

Archeologists cite the effect of this volcanic mulch in purported in-migration to the area. Several major settlements were established or expanded in this posteruption period, including the extraordinarily well-preserved ruins of Walnut Canyon and Wupatki. (See lower color insert on page C-8.) Reportedly, an estimated 1,000 Hohokam settlers migrated in from the south and similar numbers of Anasazi moved down from the north. The effects of the in-migration showed up in the culture of the Sinagua, including the distinctive pottery, cremation burials, shell jewelry, and ball courts of the Hohokam. Many archeologists argue that the Sinagua culture flourished after the eruptions, nurtured by this inflow of trade, ideas, and settlers, a dramatic example of the intimate connection between civilization and geology—even the geology of cataclysm.

Of course, scientists live to debate such complex points. Archeologist Peter Pilles, Jr., in his book *Earth Fire* argues that the volcanic mulch has been given too much credit for the population boom around the base of Humphreys Peak following the Sunset Crater eruptions. He notes that although ponderosa pine trees do now grow 1,000 feet (300 m) lower in the ashfall zone than in other areas, they are often smaller than normal, with many crooked and bent branches. Instead of the insulating effect of a layer of ash, Pilles points to generally increased rainfall in the decades after the eruptions. The ashfall may have played a role in the driest areas, but the population boom affected areas outside the ashfall as well, Pilles argues. But whether as a result of an increase in rainfall or the ash layer or some combination of those factors, the population of the region around Humphreys Peak boomed in the centuries after the volcanic field fell silent once more. The great molten pool of magma remained 30 or 50 miles (50–80 km) beneath the surface, but the violence

These 800-year-old ruins testify to the complex connection between mountains and human beings. The explosion of the volcano that sits at the heart of Sunset Crater National Monument 1,000 years ago initially proved devastating to people living nearby. However, the layer of volcanic mulch left behind actually increased the growing season in the area leading to a population boom and the construction of these ruins at Wupatki National Monument. *(Peter Aleshire)*

The snowcapped peaks of the San Francisco Mountains rise from the grasslands near Flagstaff, Arizona. Formed by a volcano that ultimately blew its top off, the peaks are sacred to many Native American tribes who live in the region, including the Hopi, Navajo, and Havasupi. *(Peter Aleshire)*

of the eruption that had covered 800 square miles (2,070 km²) with ash had settled the magma chambers into a period of quiet likely to last for thousands of years.

The Sinagua built new settlements—many much more elaborate than the earlier pit house villages. They left behind some of the most interesting and beautiful ruins in the Southwest built atop that seemingly catastrophic ash layer. That includes Wupatki, protected now as a national monument adjacent to Sunset Crater. The settlement housed several hundred people, living in masterfully fitted together two- and three-story buildings made from sandstone blocks. It includes a beautifully preserved ball court, where people gathered for ceremonial games in the style of the great civilizations of Mesoamerica. Near the ruin is a geological blowhole, from which a constant strong wind issues. The small fissure at the surface connects to a complex network of caves and cracks in the layers of limestone below. The limestone is composed of the skeletons of microscopic marine creatures that settled into the mud at the bottom of a long-vanished inland sea, then deeply buried and compressed into a layer of stone. Groundwater dissolved the limestone along fracture lines, creating a hidden network of voids and caves. In periods of high atmospheric pressure like the winter, the blowhole sucks in air. In periods of lower atmospheric pressure, as in the summer, the air rushes back out of the blowhole. The location of this probably sacred site may have influenced the placement of Wupatki, as did the temporary bounty of the heat and moisture-harboring ashfall. However, the Sinagua in the 1400s mysteriously abandoned Wupatki and all the other stone villages they built so laboriously throughout the region, just before the arrival of the Spanish in North and Central America. The abandonment of settlements across the Southwest remains one of the great archeological missing-persons cases of all time. Researchers have worked for decades to understand what happened.

Some suspect conflict between different cultures. In the decades before the abandonment, many people withdrew from vulnerable, unwalled settlements near their fields and built great pueblos in inaccessible and easily defended places. Although few of the ruins have any obvious signs of warfare, many archeologists believe that only fear of attack could have prompted so many people to build such obvious fortresses.

However, most researchers suggest that a combination of overpopulation, the exhaustion of local resources, climate shifts, and the resulting collapse of regional trade networks might have simply made life too hard to sustain the large settlements in an arid region. Although the abandonment in the 1400s does not coincide with a single, regionwide *drought*, a series of smaller-scale, sometimes severe droughts probably played a role in destabilizing the whole system. The population boom around Humphreys Peak caused by even the small advantage offered by an insulating ash layer demonstrate how close to the edge of survival many of the cultures of the Southwest existed.

CLUES TO A VANISHED PEOPLE

So what happened to the Sinagua? Where did they go? Once again, the eruption of Sunset Crater provides an important clue. Just north of the Sunset Crator area, the Hopi live on a series of high, flat-topped mesas. They had already lived on top of those mesas for a long time when Francisco Coronado's expedition in search of the fabled Seven Cities of Gold encountered them in 1540. The Hopi have since become master weavers and potters who cling steadfastly to ancient traditions on their 2.5 million-square-mile (6.5-million-km²) reservation. Their reservation includes a village established in 169 B.C.E. that is the oldest continuously inhabited place in North America. Some 7,000 Hopi now live on the reservation, trying to preserve their traditional beliefs and eke out a living from tourism, arts, and farming.

The Hopi have long claimed a connection to the Sinagua and the other pueblo-building people of that vanished era. They reject all of the names of the archeologists for those vanished cultures, referring to them all as Hisatsinom, which means "ancient people." The Hopi trace some of their clans to specific sites from that era and believe that many of the groups which lived scattered across the Southwest ended up moving to the Hopi mesas, including a number of clans that connect their origins to Humphreys Peak and the region around Sunset Crater, some 65 miles (105 km) to the south. The connection to that titanic series of eruptions and to the Sinagua who lived among the cinder cones comes in the form of myth, several elaborate Hopi stories that seem to recall the time of the eruptions.

One story holds that people living in one of the Hopi villages grew greedy and half-crazed because of their out-of-control gambling. The headman or spiritual leader of the village saw that his people had become *koyaanisqatsi*, or "crazy without regard to human life and values." So he set out to visit the supernatural beings—the kachina spirits also known as Yaayapontsam, who lived on top of Humphreys Peak. These deities, with special control over wind and fire, sent a firestorm racing across the desert to destroy the wicked village.

Another more elaborate story is recounted in *Earth Fire* by Ekkehart Malotki and Michael Lomatuway'ma. They say a spirit being, a Ka'nas kachina, who came down from Humphreys Peak in the form of a young man and fell in love with a beautiful girl he found grinding corn in one of the Hopi villages. The rich and complex story recounts their courtship and their journey on a rainbow to Humphreys Peak. Here, he revealed his true nature. She survived many dangerous tests set to her by the other kachinas, thanks to the help and intervention of Old Spider Woman, the protective spirit of the Hopi. The young kachina then returned with the beautiful girl to the village, where he married her amidst great rejoicing. After that, his power ensured prosperity for the tribe, bringing abundant rainfall and tall fields of corn.

However, human beings are contrary and quarrelsome and some wicked people in the village resented the young kachina and the good fortune of his wife and her family. In the tale, these wicked and envious people are called the "turds." So one of them who was the same size as the young man waited until the kachina went away on a trip, then came to his wife in the middle of the night. In the darkness, he pretended to be her husband. Fooled by his mask, she slept with him. When the kachina returned, his powers immediately revealed to him what the turds had done. Angered and saddened, the kachina withdrew his protection and favor from the village. He warned them that they must now pray very hard for rain, but even so they could not be sure of it. Then he returned to Humphreys Peak and his home with the kachinas. But the betrayal of the turds preyed on him, especially when he realized that no one in the village had warned his wife or protected her from the treachery of the wicked men. Finally he grew so angry that he resolved to destroy the village. Fortunately, his relatives convinced him instead to just give them a bad scare. So he made a hole in the top of a mountain and filled it with snakeweed and pine needles and pinesap. He set it alight and blew on it until he was dizzy with the effort. Then he went into a large cavern and implored the Whirlwind to make the fire hotter and blow it towards the wicked village, to teach those turds a lesson. So the Whirlwind came and blew on the fire, making it furious and hot. But the kachina had made a mistake. He had dug the hole in the top of the mountain too deep. And now the fire was so hot that it burned down through the rock, down into the Earth where other spirits lived and tended terrible underground fires. So the fire from the top of the mountain burned down until it found that other deeper earth fire. Now the fire flared back up through the mountain, hotter than ever, so that even the kachinas feared the result. The mountain gushed fire and molten embers, which fell on every side, setting everything on fire. The molten embers rose up so high they flowed out of the hole in the top of the mountain, then ran down the hill straight towards the village where the turds cowered in fear. But seeing that his demonstration had gotten entirely out of control, the kachina pleaded with the Whirlwind to stop the rushing flow of molten rock. So they ran together along the front of the lava flow, blowing on it to cool it and make it stop. They managed to stop the lava before it destroyed everything, including the village of the turds. Even so, the evil men did not escape the revenge of the kachinas. The spirits inflicted a drought on the people of the village, so that every year for four years their crops withered in the field. Each year, more and more of the people suffered from sickness and starvation. But curiously enough, only the turds actually died. When they had all died away, the kachinas took pity on the village and let the rains return.

This long and interesting Hopi myth thus precisely describes the cataclysmic eruptions that took place some 800 years ago, a remarkable example of both the persistence of an oral culture and the impact of geological forces on human societies. In the process, it confirms the theory that the Sinagua never vanished—the survivors of ecological and climate change simply moved to the Hopi mesas and continued telling the stories that had guided them for all the centuries past. And somewhere, 50 miles (80 km) beneath the surface, the earth fires still burn, waiting for the next time human foolishness—or a crack in the Earth—unleashes them once again.

Glossary

algae plant or plantlike organisms that generally live in water and generate energy from solar energy using chlorophyll, including green, yellow-green, brown, and red algae in the eukaryotes and especially formerly the cyanobacteria in the prokaryotes

archeology the scientific study of past human life and activities through the examination of fossil relics, artifacts, and monuments

atmosphere the gaseous envelope of a planet or the whole mass of air surrounding the Earth

avalanche a large mass of snow, ice, earth, rock, or other material in swift motion down a mountainside. Also a sudden overwhelming rush or accumulation of something

basalt a common gray to black volcanic rock. Normally rapid cooling at the surface makes it fine-grained

caldera a volcanic crater formed by collapse of the central part of a volcano or by very violent explosions

carbonate a salt or ester of carbonic acid

carbon dating the determination of the age of old material by using the relative content of carbon 14, an element taken up in different ratios by living things

carbon dioxide a colorless gas comprise of one carbon and two oxygen atoms that does not support combustion, dissolves in water to form carbonic acid, forms in animal respiration and in decayed organic matter, and is absorbed from the air by plants in photosynthesis

Cascades Range a chain of mountains in the western United States. A continuation of the Sierra Nevadas, the Cascades extend north from Lassen Peak across Oregon and Washington

cataclysm a great disaster, often natural

cinder cone a cone-shaped hill or mountain formed when lava and ash shoot out of a vent and fall back to form a symmetrical mound

convection the circulatory motion that occurs in a heated fluid due to the variation of its density and the action of gravity

Cretaceous the last period of the Mesozoic era characterized by continued dominance of reptiles and angiosperms, plus the diversification of mammals, and the extinction of many types of organisms at the close of the period

Devonian   the period of the Paleozoic era between the Silurian and the Mississippian

DNA   any of various nucleic acids that carry inherited genetic information. The strand of DNA which includes some 30,000 genes in human beings forms a double helix held together by hydrogen bonds between purine and pyrimidine bases which project inward from two chains containing alternate links of deoxyribose and phosphate

dome   an upward fold in rock whose sides dip uniformly in all directions

dormant   sleeping or inactive, as in a volcano that has not erupted in a long time but still might

drought   a period of significantly below-average rain

East Pacific Rise   a long undersea chain of volcanic mountains that forms on the boundary between two crustal plates

fissure   a narrow opening produced by cleavage or separation of parts

geophysicists   a branch of earth science dealing with the physical processes and phenomena occurring especially in the Earth and in its vicinity

geosynclinal   a great downward flexure of the Earth's crust

glaciologist   a scientist who studies glaciers

Global Positioning System   space-based radio-navigation system that broadcasts pinpoint navigation pulses to users on or near the Earth

Gondwana (Gondwanaland)   hypothetical land area believed to have once connected the Indian subcontinent and the landmasses of the Southern Hemisphere

Great Rift Valley   a depression in Southwest Asia and East Africa that extends with several breaks from valley of Jordan River south to central Mozambique. The rift may be the start of the formation of a new ocean basin

greenhouse gases   molecules of gases like carbon dioxide and methane that pose little barrier to incoming solar radiation, but block infrared radiation coming from the heated surface. Such gasses tend to trap solar radiation in the lower atmosphere and so cause a greenhouse effect

guyot   a flat-topped mountain in the ocean named for Swiss geologist Arnold H. Guyot who died 1884

hot spot   a stationary spot on the Earth's surface that generates volcanic activity for so long that crustal plates move past it and the volcanic activity generates a chain of islands or craters as in the creation of the Hawaiian Islands

hydroelectric   relating to production of electricity by waterpower

hypothermia   subnormal temperature of the body

jet stream   a narrow meandering current of high-speed winds near the tropopause blowing from a generally westerly direction and often exceeding a speed of 250 miles (402 kilometers) per hour

Jurassic   the period of the Mesozoic era between the Triassic and the Cretaceous during which both birds and dinosaurs first appeared

Laurasia a hypothetical land area though to have connected the land-masses of the northern hemisphere, with the exception of the Indian subcontent

lava bombs blobs of molten rock ejected from a volcano

limestone a rock formed chiefly by buildup of organic remains such as shells or coral that consists mainly of calcium carbonate

lithosphere the outer part of the solid Earth composed of rock consisting of the crust and outermost layer of the mantle, and usually considered to be about 60 miles (100 kilometers) in thickness

magma molten rock material within the Earth from which igneous rocks form when they cool

magma chamber an area beneath a volcano where molten rock builds up under pressure before it escapes to the surface

mantle the part of the interior of a planet that lies beneath the crust and above the central core

Mogollon Rim a line of uplifted cliff that cuts across Arizona and forms the southern edge of the Colorado Plateau

oceanic crust differs from the crust of the continents in that it is thinner, denser, younger, and of a different chemical composition. It is generally formed at the spreading centers of oceanic ridges, while continental crust usually forms above subduction zones

Ordovician the period between the Cambrian and the Silurian or the corresponding system of rocks

orogeny the process of mountain formation, especially by folding of the Earth's crust

paleontology a science dealing with the life of past geological periods as known from fossil remains

Paleozoic an era of geological history that extends from the beginning of the Cambrian to the close of the Permian marked by high point of nearly all classes of invertebrates, except insects

plateaus a usually extensive land area having a relatively level surface raised sharply above adjacent land on at least one side

pluton a large body of intrusive igneous rock

pulverize to reduce by crushing, beating, or grinding into very small particles

pyroclastic formed by or involving fragmentation as a result of volcanic or igneous action

Quechua a family of languages spoken by Indian peoples of Peru, Bolivia, Ecuador, Chile, and Argentina

radioactivity the property possessed by elements like uranium and isotopes like carbon 14 by which they spontaneously emit energetic particles like electrons or alpha particles as a result of the disintegration of their atomic nuclei

rhyolite a very acid volcanic rock that is the lava form of granite

rifts great fissures or crevasse or sunken zones that form along fault systems, usually along the boundary between two crustal plates

San Andreas Fault   a major zone of deep fractures extending from the Gulf of California through the length of California and into the seafloor off the Pacific Northwest. Movement of the tectonic plates along the fault has caused many earthquakes, including the massive San Francisco quake of 1906

schist   a type of metamorphic rock generally formed by reheating under pressure buried sedimentary layers of clay and mud. Schist rocks include often-flaky, layered minerals such as micas, chlorite, talc, hornblende, graphite, and others

sediment   the matter that settles to the bottom of a liquid or is deposited by water, wind, or glaciers

shale   fissile rock formed by the consolidation of clay, mud, or silt. Shale has a finely stratified or laminated structure and is made from minerals unaltered since deposition

shield volcano   a broad, rounded volcano built up by successive outpourings of very fluid lava

subduction   the process in plate tectonics in which the edge of one crustal plate descends below the edge of another

succulent   a plant with fleshy tissues that conserve moisture

transform faults   a strike-slip fault usually between segments of a mid-ocean ridge or other tectonic-plate boundary characterized by shallow high-magnitude earthquakes, like the San Andreas Fault

Triassic   the earliest period of the Mesozoic era marked by the first appearance of the dinosaurs

undersea trench   a deep rift that forms on the seafloor where one crustal plate is forced down beneath another

volcano   vent in the crust of the Earth or another planet or a moon from which usually molten or hot rock and steam issue. Also a hill or mountain composed wholly or in part of the ejected material

Books

Allen, Ian. *Snowcaps on the Equator*. London: The Bodley Head, 1988. Fine photographs and a brief description of most of the major aspects of the Kilimanjaro.

Armington, Stan. *Trekking in the Nepal Himalaya*. Oakland, Calif.: Lonely Planet, 1994. Informative guide to travel in the Himalayas.

Bass, Dick, and Frank Wells with Rick Ridgeway. *Seven Summits*. New York: Warner Books, 1986. Absorbing account of the obsessive effort to climb to the high point on each of the seven continents.

Bibby, Brian. *An Ethnographic Evaluation of Yosemite Valley: The Native American Cultural Landscape*. Report prepared for U.S. Department of the Interior, Yosemite National Park, 1994.

Carson, Rob. *Mount St. Helens: The Eruption and Recovery of a Volcano*. Seattle: Sasquatch Books, 2002. A fascinating book that examines not only the 1980 eruption, but also the slow but steady recovery of the community.

Cyancara, Alan. *Bare Bones Geology: For the Geologically Challenged*. London: Trafford Publishing, 2001. Good basic primer on the key concepts and theories that have shaped geology.

Fisher, James F. *Sherpas: Reflections on Change in Himalayan Nepal*. Berkeley: University of California, 1990. An interesting but sometimes dry account of the changes that have faced the Sherpas who make the extreme-adventure tourist industry that gets people to the top of Everest, with sometimes fatal results.

Gary, Ken and Malotki, Ekkehart. *Earth Fire: A Hopi Legend of the Sunset Crater Eruption*. Flagstaff, Ariz.: Kiva Publishing, 2005.

Grant, Glen. *Hawaii: The Big Island: A Visit to a Realm of Beauty, History and Fire*. London: Mutual Publishing, 1989. A beautifully illustrated book that surveys the geology, mythology, and history of Hawaii's volcanoes.

Hastenrath, S. *The Glaciers of Equatorial East Africa*. AH Dordrecht, The Netherlands: D. Reidel Publishing Company, 1984. A dense but informative discussion of glaciers in tropical Africa, close to the equator.

Hill, Mary. *Geology of the Sierra Nevada*. Berkeley: University of California Press, 2006. Excellent, sometimes technical, account of the forging of the Sierra Nevadas and the impact of the mountain range on the history of the region.

Hornbein, Thomas F. *Everest: The West Ridge.* San Francisco: The Sierra Club, 1966. Interesting account of an Everest route less taken.

Huber, N. King. *The Geologic Story of Yosemite National Park.* Yosemite: Yosemite Association, 1987. Short, clear, and peerless pocket guide for the layman and professional.

King, Philip B. *The Evolution of North America.* Princeton, N.J.: Princeton University Press, 1977. Technical but comprehensive account.

Krakauer, Jon. *Into Thin Air.* New York: First Anchor Books, 1999. A must-read account of the single most disastrous climbing season in the history of Everest.

Lamb, Simon. *Devil in the Mountain: A Search for the Origin of the Andes.* Princeton, N.J.: Princeton University Press, 2004. A fascinating account of an adventurous geologist's attempt to unravel the mysteries of the Andes origins.

MacDougall. J. D. *A Short History of the Planet Earth: Mountains, Mammals, Fire and Ice.* New York: Wiley & Sons, 1998. A good sweeping introduction to the most important theories on the formation and evolution of the Earth.

McBride, L. R. *About Hawaii's Volcanoes.* London: Petroglyph Press, Ltd., 1986. Basic and perhaps dated, this book gives a clear overall account with good images and graphics.

McPhee, John. *Assembling California.* New York: Farrar, Straus and Giroux, 1994. A fascinating ramble through the Sierras and other key places in California in the company of an expert science writer who weaves together the natural, geological, and human history of the region.

———. *Basin and Range.* New York: Farrar, Straus and Giroux, 1982. Fascinating account by one of the most passionate and readable popular writers on geology.

Messner, Reinhold. *The Crystal Horizon: Everest—The First Solo Ascent.* Seattle: The Mountaineers, 1989. An interesting account that shows how much things have changed—and not changed—on the world's highest mountain.

Muir, John. *My First Summer in the Sierra.* San Francisco: Sierra Club Books. 1990. Reprint of conservationist John Muir's first vivid and passionate account of his time in the Sierra Nevadas. His writing style seems breathless and exaggerated to modern ears, but he launched the modern conservationist movement.

Piers, Paul Read. *Alive.* New York: Avon Books, 1974. A best-selling account of the desperate struggle to survive high atop the Andes by a group of people who survived a plane crash on a remote peak.

Reader, John. *Kilimanjaro.* New York: University Books, 1982. A beautiful coffee table format book, it includes an account of the history of the mountain and the writer's trips.

Rhodes, Frank. *Geology*. New York: St. Martin's Press, 2001. An entry in the publisher's long-standing Golden series, this book offers a good basic explanation of geology and the evolution of the planet.

Ridgeway, Rick. *The Shadow of Kilimanjaro*. New York: Henry Holt and Company, 1999. An engaging account of the author's wanderings through the Kilimanjaro region, including his encounters with wildlife and varied cultures.

Stedman, Henry. *Kilimanjaro: A Trekking Guide to Africa's Highest Mountain*. Surrey, Eng.: Trailblazer Publications, 2003. An engaging guide to climbing Kilimanjaro, with interesting tidbits about the history of the mountain and its people.

Tabor, R. W. *Geology of the North Cascades: A Mountain Mosaic*. Seattle: Mountaineers Books, 1999. An interesting, although sometimes technical, look at the geology of the chain of volcanoes that make up the Cascades.

Thordarson, Thor, and Armann Hoskuldsson. *Iceland*. London: Terra Publishing, 2002. A sometimes technical but comprehensive and rewarding account of the strange geology of Iceland.

Thybony, Scott. *A Guide to Sunset Crater and Wupatki*. Washington, D.C.: National Parks Association, 1987. A comprehensive and readable guide to the geology, natural history, and cultures of the Sunset Crater area.

Weidensaul, Scott. *Mountains of the Heart: A Natural History of the Appalachians*. New York: Fulcrum Publishing, 2000. A comprehesive natural history of the mountain range.

Wielochowski, Andrew. *East Africa International Mountain Guide*. London: EWP, 1986. Selected walking and climbing route descriptions.

Web Sites

Earthguide: Descent to Mid-Atlantic Ridge
http://earthguide.ucsd.edu/mar/
Interesting site put up by Scripps Institute of Technology about an expedition in a submersible to the Mid-Atlantic Ridge

National Geographic News
http://news.nationalgeographic.com/news/2003/09/0923_030923_
kilimanjarogla ciers.html
National Geographic has an interesting and varied Web site that can offer wonderful images and information on many topics—including this article about the crumbling glaciers of Kilimanjaro

National Park Service: Wupatki
http://www.nps.gov/wupa/
Park Service Web sites provide good basic information and useful links, in this case to an exploration of Wupatki National Monument near the base of the San Francisco Peaks in Arizona

National Park Service: Yosemite
http://www.nps.gov/archive/yose/home.htm
This Web site provides lots of interesting information and useful links to topics about Yosemite National Park and other sites in the Sierra Nevada.

PBS-TV: NOVA ONLINE
http://www.pbs.org/wgbh/nova/everest
Excellent Web site by the PBS television program NOVA on Mount Everest and various climbing disasters

Science Daily
http://www.sciencedaily.com/encyclopedia/Geology_of_the_Alps/
This Web site compiles and updates science articles from many sources. Check out this article about the Alps, but use the search window to check out other topics. The site includes excellent science articles about most of the mountains in this book

A Teacher's Guide to the Geology of Hawaii Volcanoes National Park
http://volcano.und.edu/vwdocs/vwlessons/atg.html
Good lesson planning material and basic information on Hawaii's volcanoes offered by the Hawaii Natural History Association

U.S. Geological Survey: Cascades Volcano Observatory, Vancouver, Washington
http://vulcan.wr.usgs.gov/Volcanoes/MSH
Mount Saint Helens photographs and current conditions from the United States Geological Survey Web site

U.S. Geological Survey: Description of Mount Saint Helens
http://USGS.gov
Excellent images and discussion of the Saint Helens eruption and its aftermath

U.S. Geological Survey: The Geologic Provinces of the United States
http://www2.nature.nps.gov/geology/usgsnps/province/appalach.html.
Excellent United States Geological Service Web site on the evolution of the Appalachians. Once on this site, you can find interesting material on most of the mountains featured in this book

U.S. Geological Survey: The Geologic Story of Yosemite Valley
http://geology.wr.usgs.gov/docs/usgsnps/yos/topobk.html
The site offers a wealth of information about Yosemite. This is just a starting point, since it connects to many Web pages with information plus the USGS digital library, with hundreds of historic photos of the park and other sites in the Sierra Nevadas

U.S. Geological Survey: Volcanoes and History: Cascade Range Volcano Names
http://vulcan.wr.usgs.gov/LivingWith/Historical/volcano_names.html
Good overview of the mountains of the Cascades Range

Biological Sciences, Santa Barbara City College, Marine Science
http://www.biosbcc.net/ocean/marinesci/02ocean/hwgeo.htm
This marine science Web site has lots of great pictures of Hawaii and its volcanoes and some interesting general information

Index

Note: *Italic* page numbers indicate illustrations.
C indicates color insert pages.

A

`a`a (Hawaiian lava flow) 84
Abd'l Fida 110
Acadian orogeny 29
Aconcagua 70
Adams, Mount 94, 97
Aegir Ridge 51
Africa. *See also* Kilimanjaro, Mount
  age of exploration in 111–113
  Great Rift Valley and 108–110, *109*
  human origins in 110, 116–117
Alaska 40, 94, 104, C-7
Alder Creek 56
Aleutian Islands 36, 99
Aleutian Trench 82, 83–84
algae in Lake Tahoe 67
Allegheny orogeny 29
Alps 31–41, C-2
  cataclysms of 32
  climate change and 78
  formation of 32–37
  glaciers and 38–40, 104
  global warming and 39–40
  high points of 32
  historical impact of 31–32
  hypererosion of 37–38
  snow pack losses in 40
  streams of 38
altitude sickness, on Mount Everest 6
American history, Appalachians and 15, 26–28
Anasazi 118, 121
Andes 70–78
  abrupt rise of 71–75
  ancient civilization of 70, 72, 75–77
  average height of 70
  carbonate rocks of 73–74
  and climate 70, *74*, 74–75
  elevation change in 70
  formation of 37, 70, 71–75
  glaciers and 70, 77–78, 104

global warming and 40, 77–78
Lake Titicaca 70
length of 70–71
mantle mystery and 72–74
parallel ridges of 71, 72
rain shadow desert of *74*, 74–75
snow pack losses in 40, 77–78
volcanoes of *71*, 72–73, C-4
Annapurna avalanche 7–8
Antarctica, drift of 35
Apennines, Hannibal's crossing of 40
Appalachian Plateau 16
Appalachians 14–30, C-1
  Africa and 19, 21–24, 42–43
  erosion of *14*, 15, 25–26, *27*
  Europe and 19
  high point of 14, 28–30
  historical impact of 15, 26–28
  length and height of 14
  mountain-building periods of 28–29
  mystery of 15–18
  origin and evolution of 15–26, 28–29, 36,
    42–43
  parallel chain of 15–16
  sections of 16
  streams of *14*, 25–26, *27*
Apulian plate 36
Aqaba, Gulf of 108
Arabia, split from Africa 108
Arctic Ocean 49
Arizona. *See* Humphreys Peak
Asia. *See also* Everest, Mount
  glacier retreat in 104
asteroid, and dinosaur extinction 36
asthenosphere 73
astronomy, Mauna Kea use in 86–87
Atacama Desert *74*
Atacama Trench 71–72
Atahualpa (Inca ruler) 77
Atlantic Ocean 35. *See also* Mid-Atlantic Ridge
Atlantic Plain 25
Atlas Mountains, Appalachians and 19, 21–24,
    42–43

Atwater, Tanya 98–99
Australia, drift of 35
Austria, glacier retreat in 104
avalanche, Annapurna 7–8

B

Baker, Mount 97
Bangladesh, global warming and 40
basalt 2–3, 22, 47, 116
Basket Dome 57
batholith, Sierra Nevada 59
Battle of Lake Trasimene 40
Beaumont, Jean-Baptiste Élie de 16
Beidleman, Neil 4–7
Bering Strait land bridge 20
Bible, great flood of 16
Bilham, Roger 11
Bill Williams Mountain 116
Black Mountains 28–30
Blanc, Mont 32
Blue Ridge 16
Boukreev, Anatoli 4–8
Bridalveil Falls 59
Bridge of the Gods 94
British settlement of America 26–28
Byrd Polar Research Center 105

C

Calaveras Skull 65–66
caldera 59, 62, 83
California. *See* Sierra Nevada
California Trail 55–56
Cannae, Hannibal's victory at 40–41
cannibalism, by Donner Party 55–56
carbonate rocks, of Andes 73–74
carbon dating, in Andes 78
carbon dioxide, and climate change 29, *106*
Carlsberg Ridge *81*
Carson, Kit 67
Carter, Jimmy 93
Carthage, conflict with Romans 31, 40–41
Cascades Range
    Crater Lake 67, 97
    glacier retreat and loss 104
    Klickitat legend of 94
    magnetism and 93, 96–98
    Mount Saint Helens 89–99
    plate tectonics and 89–91, 96–99
    snow pack losses in 40
    volcanic history of 94–96
    volcanic mountains of 97
Castle Creek period, of Mount Saint Helens 95
cataclysms
    Alps 32
    Hawaiian 80
    Humphreys Peak 115–1`7, 125
    Mount Saint Helens 91, 94
Central Valley of California 58, 66
Chagga people 110

Challenger 44
Chamberlain, C. Page 62–63
Chile Trench *81*, C-4
China, glacier retreat in 104
cinder cone 87, 115, 117–121
Climb, The (Boukreev) 8
climbing
    Mount Everest 4–10, 12
    Mount Kenya 112
    Mount Kilimanjaro 111–113
Clingman, Thomas 30
Coast Ranges, snow pack losses in 69
Coldwater Ridge 91
collision of plates 2–3. *See also* plate tectonics
Colorado Plateau 115
Colorado River, erosive power of 38
Columbia River 91–95
Columbia River Gorge 94
Columbus, Christopher 48
conservation movement 59, 65–66
continental crust 2–3, *34*. *See also* plate tectonics
continental drift 20–21
    and Alps 32–37
    and Andes 72
    and Appalachians 21–26
    and Himalayas 10–13
    and hot spots 49–52
    and Mid-Atlantic Ridge 42–47, 49–52
    and Sierra Nevada 58–59, 61–62
convection
    and Hawaii 82
    and hot spots 51, 82
    and mantle 73
    and Mid-Atlantic Ridge 46, 51
    and plate tectonics 22, 32
Cook, James 87
cooling theory of mountain origin 1–2, 16–18,
        43–44
core-mantle boundary *81*
Coronado, Francisco 124
Cougar stage, of Mount Saint Helens 95
Cowlitz River 91
Crater Lake 67, 97
Cretaceous period, and Mount Everest 35

D

Dana, James Dwight 17–18
Deccan Traps 36
Desaguadero River 70
Devonian period 29
Diamond Head 85
dissected plateaus *17*
Diving Board *xiv*
DNA 110, 116–117
"Dolphin Rise" 45
dome, of Mount Saint Helens 95, C-6
Donner, George 55–56
Donner, Jacob 55
Donner Lake 56

Donner Party 55–56
dormant volcanoes 82
double continent collision *34*
Durham, University of 51

E

Earth Fire (Pilles) 122, 125
earthquakes
  Hawaiian 86
  Himalayan monitoring for 9
  Mount Saint Helens and 89, 91
  plate tectonics and 3, 46
  Sierra Nevada and 59
  and Lake Tahoe 67
East Pacific Rise 72, *81*, 98
El Capitan 61, 64
Elden Mountain 117
Eldfell (Icelandic volcano) 53–54
Emerson, Ralph Waldo 66
Eric the Red 48
Eriksson, Leif 48
erosion
  of Alps 37–38
  of Appalachians *14*, 15, 25–26, *27*
  of Mount Kenya 112
  of Mount Kilimanjaro 108
  of Sierra Nevada 63–64
Europe. *See* Alps
European history, Alps and 31–32, 40–41
Everest, George 44
Everest, Mount 4–13
  altitude sickness on 6
  "death" or "kill" zone of 5, 8
  deaths on 5
  Fischer (Scott) and Hall (Ron) expeditions 4–7
  formation of 10–13, 35–36
  Hillary (Edmund) and Tenzing Norgay summit
    of 8
  Hillary's (Edmund) criticism of climbs 8–10
  Mallory (George Leigh) disappearance on 12
  mass of 44
  revenue from climbs 5
  Sharp's (David) death on 8
  Sherpas and 7, 8
exfoliation of granite 63–64

F

Farallon Plate 98–99
fault block mountains *17*
First Step of Everest 12
Fischer, Scott 4–8
fissures 2
  and Alps 35
  and Andes 72
  and Appalachians 23
  and Cascades Range 90–91, 96–97
  and Humphreys Peak 120
  and Iceland 51
  and Mount Kilimanjaro 108

fjords of Iceland 53, C-*2*
Flagstaff, Arizona 115–117
folded mountains *17*
formation of mountains 1–3, *34*
  Alps 32–37
  Andes 37, 70, 71–75
  Appalachians 15–26, 28–29, 42–43
  biblical theory of 16
  cooling theory of 1–2, 16–18, 43–44
  geosynclinal theory of 17–18
  Himalayas 10–13, 35–36
  Mid-Atlantic Ridge 42–47
  Mount Kilimanjaro 100–102, 108–110
  plate tectonic theory of 2–3, 21–22, 42–44
  Sierra Nevada 57–59
  volcanoes and 2–3, 84–85
France, glacier retreat in 104
Fremont, John C. 67
French and Indian War 26
French settlement of America 26–28
Furtwängler Glacier 105

G

Gairdner, Meredith 95
Galápagos Islands, as hot spot 82–83
Garibaldi, Mount 97
Geological Survey of Norway 51
geophysicists 51, 73
Georgia Institute of Technology 50
geosynclinal 17–18
geothermal energy, on Iceland 52–53
geyser, Icelandic 52–53
giant sequoias 66, 67–69
Gibbs, Mount 30
Gibralter, Rock of 19
Gibralter, Strait of 37
Glacier Peak 97
glaciers
  and Alps 38–40, 104
  anatomy of *103*
  and Andes 70, 77–78, 104
  features of *103*
  formation of 104
  and Hawaii 80, 86
  and Humphreys Peak 117
  and Iceland 53, C-*3*
  and Mount Kilimanjaro 100, *101*, 102–107,
    C-*7*
  retreat and loss of 39–40, *101*, 102–107, C-*7*
  and Sierra Nevada 58, 59, 63, *64*, 64–65, 67,
    104
  and Lake Tahoe 67
  and Lake Titicaca 70
  volcanoes suppressed by 63
glaciologist 77
Global Positioning System (GPS) 9
global warming 39–40, 67, 69, 77–78, 100, *106*
Goat Rocks eruption of Mount Saint Helens 95
Gondwana (Gondwanaland) 19, 33

Grand Canyon 38, 115
granite, of Sierra Nevada 57, 59–64, C-3, C-4
Great Appalachian Valley 26
Great Basin 66
Great Lakes 104
Great Rift Valley 108–110
Great Salt Lake Desert 56
greenhouse gases 69
Greenland 49, 50, 51–52, 53
Griggs, David 46
Groom, Mike 6–7
Gulf Coast, U.S., global warming and 40
gulf coastal plain 25
Gutenberg, Beno 46
guyots 47

H

Haleakala 82, 83
Half Dome 61, 64, C-4
Hall, James 17–18
Hall, Rob 4–7
Hannibal 31, 40–41
Hanson, Doug 7
Harris, Andy 6–7
Harris, Morgan xiv
"Hastings Cutoff" 55
Haulalai 82
Havasupi 123
Hawaii 79–88
    cataclysms of 80
    core-mantle boundary at 81
    discovery and settlement of 87
    endangered native species of 87
    glaciers and 80, 86
    as hot spot 49, 79–80, 82–84
    mythology of 80–81, 87–88
    undersea landslides of 80, 81
    volcanoes of 79–88, C-5
Hawaii, Big Island of 82
Hawaiian Ridge-Emperor Seamounts 82
Heezen, Bruce 47
Hekla, Mount 52–54
Hemingway, Ernest 113
Hercynic range 33
Hetch Hetchy 58, 66
Hillary, Edmund 8–10, 12
Himalayan-type mountains 34
Himalayas 9, 11, C-1
    Annapurna 7–8
    Mount Everest 4–13
    formation of 10–13, 34, 35–36
    measurement and monitoring of 9
Hisatsinom 124
Hohokam 118, 121–122
homo sapiens 110, 116–117
Hood, Mount 94, 97
Hopi 119, 123, 124–126
hot spots
    Hawaii 49, 79–80, 82–84

Iceland 43, 47–54, 82–83
    Yellowstone National Park 49, 82–83
Hualalai 82, 83
Hudson Valley 26
human origins 110, 116–117
Humphreys Peak 114–126, C-8
    benefits of disaster 121–124
    formation of 115–117
    glaciers and 117
    mythology of 114–115
    Sinagua people of 118–126, C-8
    Sunset Crater 117–121, C-8
    vanished people of 124–126
hydroelectric power 105
hypererosion of Alps 37–38
hypothermia 6

I

Iapetus Ocean 28
ice ages
    and Alps 38–40
    and Humphreys Peak 117
    and Iceland 53
    and North America 104
    and Sierra Nevada 59, 64–65
ice lakes, Icelandic 53
Iceland 42, 47–54
    connection to Greenland 50, 53
    discovery and settlement of 48–49
    fjords of 53, C-2
    geothermal energy of 52–53
    glaciers of 53, C-3
    hot spot theory and 49–52, 82–83
    mythology of 48, 52
    supercomputer model of 50–51
    volcanoes of 48–49, 52–54
ice-worn hummocks 103
igneous rock 2–3
Incas 72, 75–77
India
    glaciers and water supply of 105
    global warming and 40, 105
    northward movement of 9, 11–13
Indian Ocean 35
Indo-Tibetan Border Police 7
Inglis, Mark 8–10
Inner Basin, of Humphreys Peak 117
Into Thin Air (Krakauer) 4–7
Irvine, Andrew "Sandy" 12
Italy
    glacier retreat in 104
    Hannibal and 31, 40–41
Izu Bonin 81

J

Japan, formation of 36
jet stream 4–5
Johnston, David A. 89, 91
Juan de Fuca Plate 96

Juan de Fuca Ridge 98
Jura Mountains 35
Jurassic period
    and Alps 35, 38
    and Sierra Nevada 58

K

kachina spirits 125–126
Kalama eruption of Mount Saint Helens 95
Kamehameha (Hawaiian chief) 87
Kashmir area 105
Katmai, Mount 94
Kaui 82
Kendrick Peak 116
Kenya, Mount 105, 108, 112
Kern Canyon 58
Kibo 101–102
Kilauea 80, 82, 83, *84*, 88, C-5
Kilimanjaro, Mount 100–113
    Abd'l Fida and 110
    age of exploration and 111–113
    climate change and 78, 100, 102–107
    climate zones of 106–107
    erosion of 108
    formation of 100–102, 108–110
    glacier retreat and loss 100, *101*, 102–107, C-7
    Hemingway (Ernest) and 113
    life zones of 107
    Meyer's (Hans) ascent of 111–112
    plate tectonics and 108–110
    Ptolemy of Alexandria and 110
    Rebmann (Johannes) and 102, 111
    as "shining mountain" 100–101
    weather system of 105–108
Kings Canyon 58
Klickitat legend, of Cascades Range 94
koyaanisqatsi 125
Krakauer, Jon 4–7
Krapf, Ludwig 111

L

lahar, of Mount Saint Helens eruption 91–93
Lakagigar, Mount 48
Lambert Glacier *101*
Lamont Geological Observatory 46
land bridges 20
landslides, undersea Hawaiian 80, 81
Lassen Peak 97
Laurasia 33
lava bombs 119
lava dome C-6
lava tubes 120–121
Leung, L. Ruby 69
Lewis and Clark expedition 95
limestone 10, 25, 33–35, 61, 123
lithosphere 73, *81*
Little Colorado River 120
Loihi 86
Lomatuway'ma, Michael 125

Long Valley Caldera 62
Loowit (Klickitat maiden) 94
Lopsang Jangbu 6, 8
Los Angeles, water supply to 58
"Lucy" 110

M

Machu Picchu 76–77
magma 2
    and Alps 35
    and Andes 72
    and Appalachians 23
    and Cascades Range 90–91, 96–97
    and Hawaii 82
    and Mount Kilimanjaro 108
magma chamber
    Mount Saint Helens 91
    Sierra Nevada 59
magnetism
    and Cascades Range 93, 96–98
    and Mid-Atlantic Ridge 22, *45*, 51–52, 96
Makalu Gao 7
Malaspina Glacier C-7
Mallory, George Leigh 12
Malotki, Ekkehart 125
Mammoth Mountains 59
mantle 2, 22, *34*
    and Alps 32
    and Andes 72–74
    boundary with core *81*
    and hot spots 49
    mapping and studying of 73
mass of mountains 44
Matthes Crest C-3
Maui 82
Mauna Kea 79–80, 82, 86–88
Mauna Loa 82, 83, 85, 88
Maury, Matthew Fontaine 44–45
Mawenzi 101
Medicine Lake 97
Mediterranean Sea, and Alps 37–38
mega-colossal eruptions 83
Merced River 62
Messinian Salinity Crisis 38
Meyer, Hans 111–112
Mid-Atlantic Ridge 21–22, 42–54, *43*
    core-mantle boundary at *81*
    dimensions of 42, 47
    discovery of 44–46
    formation of 42–47
    hot spot theory of 47–52
    Iceland as high point of 42, 47–54
    magnetism and 22, *45*, 51–52, 96
"Middle Ground" 45
Mississippi River, erosive power of 38
Mitchell, Elisha 29–30
Mitchell, Mount 14, 28–30, C-1
Mogollon Rim 115–116
Mohawk Valley 26

Mohorovicic Discontinuity (Moho) 73
Molokai 80
mountain(s). *See* specific mountains and ranges
mountain building 1–3, *34*
    Alps 32–37
    Andes 37, 70, 71–75
    Appalachians 15–26, 28–29, 42–43
    biblical theory of 16
    cooling theory of 1–2, 16–18, 43–44
    geosynclinal theory of 17–18
    Himalayas 10–13, 35–36
    Mount Kilimanjaro 100–102, 108–110
    Mid-Atlantic Ridge 42–47
    plate tectonic theory of 2–3, 21–22, 42–44
    Sierra Nevada 57–59
    volcanoes and 2–3, 84–85
mudflow, from Mount Saint Helens 91–93
Muir, John 65–66

N
Navajo *123*
Nazca Plate 72
Nevada, Sierra. *See* Sierra Nevada
Nevadan orogeny 58
New Zealand, glacier retreat in 104
North America. *See also* Appalachians; Humphreys Peak; Saint Helens, Mount; Sierra Nevada
    discovery of 48
    drift of 36
    glacier retreat in 104
North American Plate 96–99, 98–99
North Atlantic Ocean. *See* Mid-Atlantic Ridge
North Carolina Geologic Survey 29
North Dome 57
Northwestern United States. *See* Saint Helens, Mount

O
Oahu 80, 82, 85
observatories on Mauna Kea 86–87
ocean exploration 44–47
oceanic crust 2–3, *34*. *See also* plate tectonics
oceanic mountains 21–22. *See also* Mid-Atlantic Ridge
Odell, Noel 12
Ohio State University 77–78, 105
Old Spider Woman 125
Olduvai Gorge 110
Ordovician period 28–29
Owens River 58
Owens Valley 58
oxygen, Mount Everest and 4–5

P
Pacific Northwest National Laboratory 40
Pacific Ocean. *See* Hawaii
Pacific Plate 72, 82, 83–84, 98–99
pahoehoe 84

Pakistan, glaciers and water supply of 105
paleontologists 110
Pangaea
    and Alps 32–37
    and Andes 72
    and Appalachians 21–26
    and Himalayas 10–13
    and Mid-Atlantic Ridge 42–47
    Wegener's theory of 20–21, 42–43
Pele (Hawaiian goddess) 80–81, 88
Pele's Hair 81
Pele's Tears 81
Pennsylvania Dutch 26
Phyheas of Massalia 48
Piedmont 16
Piemont-Liguria Ocean 35
Pilles, Peter, Jr. 122
Pinchot, Gifford 66
Pine Creek period, of Mount Saint Helens 95
plateaus
    African 109
    Andes 75
    Icelandic 53
plate tectonics 2–3, 21–22, *34*
    and Alps 32–37
    and Andes 71–75
    and Appalachians 23–26
    and Cascades Range 89–91, 96–99
    and Himalayas 10–13
    and hot spots 49–52
    and Humphreys Peak 115–117
    and Mount Kilimanjaro 108–110
    and Mid-Atlantic Ridge 42–47, 49–52
    and Sierra Nevada 57–59, 61–62
plutons *57*, 59–64, C-4
Poliahu (Hawaiian goddess) 87–88
postshield volcanoes 85
preshield volcanoes 85
Proclamation of 1763 27–28
Ptolemy of Alexandria 110
pulverize 117
Purtscheller, Ludwig 112
pyroclastic flow, of Mount Saint Helens 91, 92

Q
Quechua 71
Quelccaya ice cap 77

R
radioactivity of rocks 22, 44, 115–116
Rainier, Mount 97
rain shadow desert 66, *68*, *74*, 74–75
Rebmann, Johannes 102, 111
Red Sea 35, 108–109
redwoods of Sierra Nevada 66, 67–69
Reed, James 55
Réunion Island, as hot spot 82–83
rhyolite 116
Richter, Charles 46

rifts
  and Alps 35
  and Appalachians 22, 24
  Great Rift Valley 108–110, *109*
  and Himalayas 10–11
  and Iceland 52–53
  and Sierra Nevada 58
Rocky Mountains 36, 40, 104, 115
Roman Empire, Alps and 31–32, 40–41
Roosevelt, Theodore 66
Russell, William H. 55

S
Saint Helens, Mount 89–99
  1980 eruption of 89–94, *90, 92,* C-6
  ash from 92, *92,* 93, C-6
  deaths in 91–93
  destruction by 91–93
  edge of blast zone *93*
  effects of *92*
  energy released in 94
  lahar of 91–93
  pyroclastic flow of 91, 92
  2004 entry into active phase 95–96
  2005 ash column of 96
  Klickitat legend of 94
  lava dome of 95, C-6
  magnetism and 93, 96–98
  plate tectonics and 89–91, 96–99
  volcanic history of 94–96
  whaleback of 96
San Andreas Fault 59, 98
Sandwich Islands 87. *See also* Hawaii
San Francisco, global warming and 40
San Francisco Peaks 118–121, *123,* C-8
Scandinavia
  snow pack losses in 40
  split from Greenland 49
scientific method 1–2
Scripps Institution of Oceanography 46, 96–97
sea level, global warming and 39–40, 105
Second Step of Everest 12
sediments 15
Sentinel Falls 59
sequoias 66, 67–69
Seven Summits 112–113
shale 25, 61
Sharp, David 8–10
Shasta, Mount 97
Shenandoah Valley 26
Sherpas 7, 8
Sherwin Glacial Period 64
shield volcanoes 85
"shining mountain" 100–101. *See also* Kiliman-
  jaro, Mount
Shipton, Eric 112
Shira 101
Sierra Club 65–66
Sierra Nevada (Spain), Appalachians and 19

Sierra Nevada (United States) 55–69
  age of 62–63
  altitude change along 66
  and climate 66
  and conservation movement 59, 65–66
  Donner Party in 55–56
  erosion of 63–64
  formation of 57–59
  giant sequoias of 66, 67–69
  glaciers and 58, 59, 63, *64,* 64–65, 67, 104
  global warming and 67, 69
  granite of *57,* 59–64, C-3, C-4
  habitats of 66–67
  high point of 58
  length of 58
  Nevadan orogeny of 58
  rainfall in, measurement of ancient 62–63
  and rain shadow desert 66, *68*
  rock masses of 61, *61,* C-3, C-4
  snow pack losses in 69
  streams of 58, 59, 62
  Lake Tahoe 58, 67
  tilt shift in 62
  waterfalls of 59, *60,* 62
  water supply from 58
  wildfires of 67–69
  Yosemite National Park *xiv, 57,* 58,
    59–69
Sierra Nevada batholith 59
Sierra Sinagua 118. *See also* Humphreys Peak
Sinagua people 118–126, C-8
Sitgreaves Mountain 116
Smoky Mountains *28*
snow pack losses 39–40, 69, 77–78, 100
sonar 21, 46–47
South America. *See also* Andes
  drift of 35
  glacier retreat in 104
South American Plate 72
South Atlantic Ocean 35
Spirit Lake 89
Spirit Lake stage, of Mount Saint Helens 95
squeeze-ups 120
stratovolcano 100–101
streams
  Alps 38
  Appalachian *14,* 25–26, *27*
  erosive power of 38
  Sierra Nevada 58, 59, 62
subduction 2–3
  and Alps 33–35
  and Appalachians 23–26
  and Cascades 99
  and Iceland 51
  and island formation 36
  and Mount Saint Helens 91
  and Sierra Nevada 58–59
Suess, Eduard 18–19, 20
Sugar Bowl period, of Mount Saint Helens 95

Sunset Crater National Monument 115, *122*
Sunset Crater phase, of Humphreys Peak
    117–121, C-*8*
Surtsey 53
Sutter's Creek 56
Sutter's Fort 56
Swift Creek stage, of Mount Saint Helens 95
Switzerland, glacier retreat in 104

T

Taconic orogeny 28
Tahoe, Lake 58, 67
Tanganyika, Lake 109
telescopes on Mauna Kea 86–87
Tenzing Norgay 8
Tethys Ocean 11–13, 35, 37
Tharp, Marie 47
Thompson, Lonnie 77–78, 105
Three Brothers 61, *61*
Tibetan Plateau 13
Tilman, Bill 112
Titicaca, Lake 70
Toutle River 91
transform faults 98, 108–109
Trasimene, Lake, Battle of 40
trenches, undersea 32, 71–72
Triassic period
    and Alps 38
    and Sierra Nevada 61–62
triple junction of plates 98–99
Truman, Harry (Mount Saint Helens resident)
    89, 91
Tuolumne River 66

U

undersea mountains 21–22. *See also* Mid-Atlantic
    Ridge
undersea trenches 32, 71–72
United States. *See* Appalachians; Humphreys
    Peak; Saint Helens, Mount; Sierra Nevada
U.S. Geological Survey 30

V

Valley and Ridge Province 16
valleys, glacier-made compared to river-made 38
vanished people of U. S. Southwest 124–126
Vatnajökull Glacier 53, C-*3*
Victoria, Lake 109
Viesturs, Ed 6
Vikings 48
Volcanic Explosivity Index 83
volcanic mulch 121–124, *122*
volcanoes
    and Andes *71*, 72–73, C-*4*

and Appalachians 15
    Cascades 97
    dormant 82
    Hawaiian 79–88, C-*5*
    and Humphreys Peak 114–126
    Icelandic 48–49, 52–54
    Mount Katmai 94
    and Mount Kilimanjaro 100–102, 108
    mega-colossal eruptions of 83
    and Mid-Atlantic Ridge 42, 47–54
    and mountain building 2–3, 84–85
    postshield 85
    preshield 85
    Mount Saint Helens 89–99
    shield 85
    and Sierra Nevada 58–59, 62, 63
    suppression by glaciers 63
    Yellowstone National Park 83

W

Walnut Canyon 121
Wasatch Mountains 56
waterfalls
    of Iceland 53
    of Yosemite 59, *60*, 62
water supply
    glacier retreat and 39–40, 104–105
    Humphreys Peak and 117
    Sierra Nevada and 58
Wegener, Alfred Lothar 19–21, 42–43
Wekiu bug 87
whaleback, of Mount Saint Helens 96
Whitney, Josiah Dwight 65–66
Whitney, Mount 58
wildfires, in Sierra Nevada 67–69
Willett, Sean 38
Wilson, Big Tom 29–30
Wilson, J. Tuzon 82, 98
Wilson, Woodrow 66
Woods Hole Oceanographic Institution 46
World Glacier Monitoring Service 104
World War II, and ocean exploration 46–47
Wupatki National Monument 121, *122*, 123, C-*8*

X

Yaayapontsam 125
Yellowstone National Park 49, 82–83
Yosemite Falls 59, *60*
Yosemite National Park *xiv*, *57*, 58, 59–69
    conservation movement and 59, 65–66
    dimensions of 59
    glaciers and 59, 63, *64*, 64–65, 67, 104
    rock masses of 61, *61*, C-*3*, C-*4*
    waterfalls of 59, *60*, 62